KUYPER IN AMERICA

D1523416

KUYPER IN AMERICA

"THIS IS WHERE I WAS MEANT TO BE"

ABRAHAM KUYPER

Edited by George Harinck

DORDT COLLEGE PRESS

These letters were translated from the Dutch by Margriet Urbanus. The original title, published in 2004 by the Historical Documentation Center for Dutch Protestantism at the VU University in Amsterdam (ISBN 90-72319-21-4), is *Ik voel steeds meer dat ik hier zijn moest: Amerikaanse brieven van Abraham Kuyper aan zijn vrouw en kinderen (1898)*.

All of the images in this volume come from the Kuyper archives at the Historical Documentation Center for Dutch Protestantism and are used with permission.

Cover design and layout by Carla Goslinga

Printed in the United States of America.

Dordt College Press   www.dordt.edu/dordt_press
498 Fourth Avenue NE
Sioux Center, Iowa 51250
United States of America

ISBN: 978-0-932914-93-4

The Library of Congress Cataloging-in-Publication Data is on file with the Library of Congress, Washington, D.C.

Library of Congress Control Number: 2012936183

TABLE OF CONTENTS

Introduction iii

Travel Schedule ix

Letters 1

Index of Names 83

INTRODUCTION

In the second half of 1898, Abraham Kuyper (1837–1920) made a journey lasting nearly five months that took him by way of England to the United States. Together with his sojourn in more southerly European regions in 1876/77, and his journey around the Mediterranean Sea in 1905/06, this American journey formed a separate chapter in Kuyper's life. He was fond of traveling and even as a young clergyman regularly crossed the nation's borders. After having overworked himself in 1876, he kept to the rule that every year during the summer months he would stay abroad for two months in order to recoup his strength.

The journey to the United States fitted into this annual pattern, albeit that upon his departure from Amsterdam on 11 August 1898, he expected, given the length of the journey, to be away for three months instead of two. This stay abroad was different from the others not only because the destination was another continent, but also because it took much longer than expected. Overwhelmed during his stay in the United States by invitations for discussions and speeches, Kuyper decided to prolong his journey, so that in the end he did not arrive back in Amsterdam until 30 December 1898. And there was still another reason why this journey was different from others he had made: his absence was not regarded as entirely proper in every respect. During his time abroad, on 6 September 1898, the inauguration of Queen Wilhelmina took place in Amsterdam, and Kuyper, being a Member of Parliament (known as the States General), was expected to attend this ceremony. Moreover, owing to his membership in the Dutch Association of Journalists, he was involved in organizing this festive occasion as the chairman of the committee responsible for receiving foreign journalists. Although Kuyper had indicated in advance that he would be staying in the United States on pressing business at the time of the inauguration, his absence strengthened the impression that he was ambivalent towards the Royal House of Orange.

What was the compelling reason to travel to the United States for a few months exactly during the late summer of 1898? Although Kuyper, who was also a professor of theology at the Free University, was not unknown in America among the circles of Dutch emigrants of Protestant descent, his name was mentioned in the 1890's more often than not by members of the Presbyterian Church. He owed a large debt of gratitude for his entry into this circle to Geerhardus Vos, professor of biblical theology at Princeton Theological Seminary in the state of New Jersey. Vos was born in the Netherlands, attended the Amsterdam *gymnasium* with Kuyper's eldest son, and then in 1881 immigrated to the United States with his parents. In 1886 Vos was notified of his appointment as professor at the Vrije Universiteit in Amsterdam, where he would be Kuyper's colleague. However, Vos turned the appointment down, choosing instead to become an instructor at the Theological School of the Christian Reformed Church, now Calvin College, in Grand Rapids, Michigan. But he did not forget Kuyper, and even before 1893, when he was appointed professor at Princeton Theological Seminary, he started to translate and publish works by Kuyper in *The Presbyterian and Reformed Review* and explain his importance to professors at Princeton like Benjamin B. Warfield as well as Francis L. Patton, who was also president of Princeton University.

As a result of becoming acquainted with Kuyper's work, the Princeton faculty decided that in 1896, on the 150th anniversary of the University's founding, Kuyper should be awarded an honorary doctorate and be invited to deliver the Stone Lectures. This was a series of lectures given annually, funded by the L. P. Stone Foundation that had been established in 1871 and was administered by the College of Professors of the Theological Seminary in Princeton. Given the many ways in which the New World had always appealed to Kuyper, and given the knowledge that he would meet many like-minded people from his native country there, the idea of crossing the ocean held great attraction for him. After postponing travel to the United States twice for various reasons, he believed he could no longer resist the pressure from the American side to be sure to come, and so he made a solemn promise to visit Princeton in 1898.

That Kuyper's journey to the United States is better known than any one of his other journeys is related to the fact that he became famous through his Stone Lectures. The *Lectures on Calvinism* were published in a Dutch edition in 1899 under the title *Het calvinisme*. In the same year an American edition of the lectures was published, followed over the years by editions in nine other languages—the book is still in print in the States and elsewhere.

Just as he would do following his journey around the Mediterranean Sea, Kuyper described his American travels in a book—*Varia Americana* (1899). In it he records his impressions of American society, its church life and political system, as well as the life of those fellow-countrymen who had immigrated to the United States. In addition to the honor bestowed upon him in Princeton, Kuyper was particularly impressed by the enthusiasm of these Dutch-Americans. The pressure that the latter group exerted on him to visit their places of settlement was an important reason to lengthen his stay in America considerably.

The present publication is an English translation of the book *Ik voel steeds meer dat ik hier zijn moest*, which came out in 2004 and contained the text of the twenty-two letters that Kuyper wrote to his wife and children from America. The collection of these sometimes hastily penned letters—including one postcard (nr. 16)—can be interpreted as the more personal companion piece to his *Varia Americana*. In addition to all sorts of domestic details, the letters discuss the same themes as in the book, but then more explicitly from a personal perspective—allowing his wife and children to share his adventures, and also his thoughts and feelings while traveling. These are typical travel letters. Things like his fatigue, the enthusiasm of his audiences, the weather, the distrust about his absence during the inauguration of Queen Wilhelmina, his motives for the trip, his command of English, his efforts to introduce the immigrants to the song *Wilhelmus* as the "Marseillaise of the Reformation," the banquets that were hosted in his honor, his growing sense of mission and the timeliness of his visit to the potential "decisive Calvinists" in America, the comparison of prices, the food, his speaking schedule, and his impressions of the great country all pass in review. Kuyper loved traveling; he basked in the official welcomes and tributes; and he enjoyed meeting many interesting people among the American elite as well as the occasional brush with common people. No door remained closed to Kuyper, not even that of the White House. But despite all these pleasures he also often felt lonely, bereft of contact with his wife and children.

For Kuyper scholars and students of American history and culture these letters contain fascinating details, and for the lover of the epistolary genre and the *petit histoire* this publication offers the opportunity to get close to the enigmatic figure of Abraham Kuyper.

The letters here published are housed in the Kuyper Archives, which is part of the collection of the Historical Documentation Centre at the VU University in Amsterdam. They belong to the personal part of the archives, which for a long time was difficult to access, if at all, but which now, thanks to a new inventory made by Margriet Urbanus, is open to researchers. Kuyper was a faithful letter-writer, and it seems that no letter is missing from his end of the correspondence between his wife and children and himself. In this way the letters form a continuous account. From the return mail a number of letters written by Mrs. Kuyper and the children to their "wandering housemate" are missing from the archives. For that reason it was decided to publish only Kuyper's letters. The ink of Kuyper's letters has not faded, but his handwriting is often poorly legible owing in part to his fatigue and emotions, as also appears from a letter his wife wrote to him on 20 October 1898: "In particular, write clearly." The context

Introduction

enabled us to establish how an occasional illegible word was to be read. As well, Kuyper's lapidary—at times telegraphic—style in these letters prompted us in a few places to add a word or two in brackets in the interest of greater clarity. Finally, glosses from *Varia Americana* that have a bearing on what Kuyper writes in his letters have been added in footnotes. For more information about Kuyper's journey to America, one may consult Peter S. Heslam, *Creating a Christian Worldview: Abraham Kuyper's Lectures on Calvinism* (Grand Rapids/Cambridge, 1998).

The editors would like to thank Dr. William Kennedy of Holland, Michigan, and Dr. Hans Krabbendam of the Roosevelt Study Center in Middelburg, the Netherlands, for the material they provided, as well as Rev. Tjitze Kuipers of Kampen, the Netherlands, who shared with them his bibliographic knowledge of Kuyper's publications in the period around 1898. They would further like to thank their colleague Professor Jan de Bruijn for his indispensable help in deciphering and interpreting Kuyper's handwriting. The translation was made by drs. Dagmare Houniet and edited by Dr. Harry Van Dyke of Redeemer University College.

George Harinck, D.Litt.
Margriet Urbanus, LL.M.
VU University
Amsterdam

Travel Schedule

August
- 11 – departs from Amsterdam
- 18 – stays in London, UK
- 20 – boards the RMS *Lucania*, Liverpool
- 27 – arrives in New York City
- 31 – visits Spring Lake Beach, New Jersey

September
- 2 – departs for the Adirondack Mountains (via the Hudson River and Albany, New York)
- 4 – in hotel in Saratoga Springs, New York
- 10 – in Keene Heights (Keene Valley), New York
- 28 – departs from Keene Heights, stays over in Elizabethtown, New York
- 29 – departs for Boston, Massachusetts

October
- 1 – departs from Boston to Hartford, Connecticut, from there to New York in the evening
- 2 – in New York City
- 3/4 – visits Princeton, New Jersey, from there back to New York
- 10/11/14 – delivers the first three Stone Lectures in Princeton
- 14 – departs for New York in the evening
- 19/20/21 – delivers the last three Stone Lectures in Princeton
- 22 – departs for New York
- 24 – departs for Detroit, Michigan
- 25 – arrives in Detroit, then travels to Grand Rapids, Michigan
- 27 – departs in the afternoon for Holland, Michigan
- 28 – tour through Vriesland, Zeeland, Drenthe, and Overijssel, Michigan
- 29 – departs for Chicago, Illinois
- 31 – departs for Pella, Iowa

November

> 2 – departs for Des Moines, Iowa
> 3 – departs for Orange City, Iowa
> 4 – departs for Chicago
> 5 – arrives in Chicago
> 7 – delivers speech in Englewood (south-side of Chicago)
> 12 – visits Pullman City and Roseland (south-side of Chicago)
> 14 – departs from Chicago, arrives in Cleveland, Ohio
> 16 – travels to Niagara Falls and subsequently to Rochester, New York
> 19/20 – departs for New York at night, arrives next morning
> [?] – delivers a speech in Paterson, New Jersey
> 28 – gives lecture in New Brunswick, New Jersey, departs for Baltimore, Maryland
> 29/30– visits Washington, D.C.

December

> 1/2/3 – visits the Dutch settlement of East Maryland
> 3 – returns to Baltimore, departs for Philadelphia, Pennsylvania at night
> 7 – lectures in Hartford, Connecticut
> 8 – returns to New York City
> 10 – departs from New York aboard the SS *Rotterdam*
> 19/20 – arrives at night in Boulogne, France, departs for London, UK
> 23 or 24 – departs for Paris, France
> 29 – departs for Brussels, Belgium
> 30 – arrives at home in Amsterdam

LETTERS

A charcoal drawing of Abraham Kuyper by Jan Veth, circa. 1892

In a limited edition of *De Standaard* that was published exclusively by the family on 1 April 1897 in a printing run of one copy, Kuyper's daughter Henriëtte described her father as a writer: "Dr. Kuyper *writes* and for him writing is the immediate outpouring of his thoughts into visible signs. No outline, no points noted in advance to show him the way. He places his piece of paper in front of him and from the amount of thoughts crowded together, all related, the ones that are called upon group themselves in such a way so as to spin out a thread that must lead to the imagined goal. As soon as his thoughts are activated, his pen ticks on the paper. At first slowly with round lettering; then, as the activity in the circle of thoughts increases, the more quickly and with smaller points and more little figures made up of dashes."

[1]

Liverpool, Hotel Adelphi
20 August 1898

My dear wife,

In a moment I will be going to the ship and will, I hope, find another message from home.[1] In London I received nothing. At least, nothing reached me. And if I receive something once I'm on board, I cannot reply anymore of course. One is not admitted on board beforehand, which can scarcely be otherwise, given some 700 to 800 passengers. I am happy to board ship at last. The bustle and warmth have tired me. This morning I tried to write a devotional, but I tore it up. I couldn't do it. Please tell *De Standaard*.[2] They will have to make do for two weeks. Yesterday Groos[3] came to the train to see me off, which I appreciated very much. I cannot get over the fact that the friends in Amsterdam let me depart so coolly. It is a wound in my heart that will not heal soon. They weren't at all busy. It is summer recess. But this too will be all right.

The weather is oppressive and foggy. Yesterday we had tremendous thunder. It will probably also be turbulent at sea. And yet I don't dread it. Of course, a voyage such as this always brings with it a certain degree of danger, but percentagewise no more than other modes of travel. Moreover, it is not a whim, but a

---

1 In 1898 the Kuyper's lived at Prins Hendrikkade 173 in Amsterdam. At that time, of their seven children, four children still lived at home (named in notes 5 through 8).

2 Reference to the editorial offices of Kuyper's antirevolutionary daily paper *De Standaard* in Amsterdam, where also his church weekly *De Heraut* was published. The devotional was meant for the latter paper.

3 Groos was a Dutch acquaintance of Kuyper who lived in Upper Norwood near London.

consequence of the stage in my life. It is the cause of my Lord that I attempt to serve also in this endeavor. Therefore, let us put our trust in Him, that He will prosper me, and pray that He will reunite us soon. You'll see, these weeks will pass quickly and be over before you know it. Many things will break up the time, not only for me but also for all of you. As far as I can gather, everything has now been arranged and put in order. Let me be without *European* worries these next few months. As soon as I arrive in America I will send you a telegram. And now, live with each other in the love and the fear of our God, to Whose care I commit you all, dear wife,[4] Bram,[5] Harry,[6] To,[7] and Jo,[8] all my darlings, together with those who are far away. Your most loving father.

---

4 Johanna Hendrika (Jo) Kuyper nee Schaay (1842–1899), wife of Abraham (Bram) Kuyper. They were married on 1 July 1863 and had eight children, of whom seven were still alive when Kuyper visited America.

5 Abraham (Bram) Kuyper, Jr. (1872–1941), Kuyper's fourth child and third son, studied theology at the Vrije Universiteit in Amsterdam and was ordained as a Reformed pastor in 1899.

6 Henriëtte Sophia Suzanna (Harry, Har) Kuyper (1870–1933), Kuyper's third child and eldest daughter. She was a freelance writer.

7 Catharina Maria Eunice (To, Tokkie) Kuyper (1876–1955), Kuyper's sixth child and youngest daughter. She worked as a nurse and was the matron of the boarding house of the Vrije Universiteit from 1927 until 1932.

8 Johanna Hendrika (Jo) Kuyper (1875–1948), Kuyper's fifth child and second daughter. She worked as a nurse.

NIEUWENDIJK Nº 89
AMSTERDAM.

Mrs. Johanna Hendrika Kuyper-Schaay, 1888

Engaged for five years, they married in July 1863. She bore him eight children. A Reformed Church pastor, C. Hunningher, who lived-in with the Kuyper family for a short time when he was younger, described her in 1922 with these words: "I was always struck by the fact that Mrs. Kuyper, even though she was her husband's kindred spirit, was kinder towards his opponents than he was." Mrs. Jo Kuyper died unexpectedly on 25 August 1899 while vacationing in Meyringen, Switzerland. She was 57 years old.

[2]

On board the RMS *Lucania* (Cunard Steamship Company)
Friday 26 August 1898

Dear wife,

Tonight at half past two we hope to moor in New York harbor, and so a short word now, in time for tonight's mail. Until now the long crossing of more than 3,000 nautical miles has been accomplished successfully under God's protection, although fog and headwinds slowed our progress. The sea was calm throughout, and the ship lay so steady on the water that I had no inclination to seasickness at all. Only the fog was disagreeable, as all accidents occur in fog, and sometimes it troubled us for 18 out of 24 hours. And then, every half minute a fog-horn cries and screams, which means that you cannot sleep at night and that by day a sense of gloom hangs over the whole ship. The distance is awesome. I never thought that this ocean was so vast. It is the distance between home and Paris *times eight*. It is also lonely. We meet almost no ships, nor follow in the wake of any. During all these days at sea I have not seen *six*. One or two whales, some flying fish, that was all, and sometimes at night a beautiful moon. My hut was very expensive and yet very small. If I had had to share it with someone else I would not have been able to move around. I have not paid much attention to the company, even at table. I felt too light-headed, the atmosphere was too oppressive, and the talking and the noise around me too loud. Luckily I have slept much during the day, have dreamt at times, and have sat in a room with a heavy head. The sea air always affects me badly.

The ship is beautiful, carrying 450 crew and having on board 800 3rd-class passengers, 300 2nd-class and 370 1st-class passengers, thus 1,900 people in all. Think of all that cooking, baking, serving all day long! As a result the food was poor. An extensive menu, but almost nothing tasty. Only the *quast*[1] with ice was good, but one had to pay extra. The people with whom I spoke (some four) did not help things. Full of Paris and sports. They are all returning from a summer holiday. After the sea voyage I feel somewhat better now. When I embarked I was completely exhausted, and that misfortune for Guy[2] made me almost despair to rush and find a pen, an envelope, and stamps. Later, after we had left shore, I read your wonderful letters calmly, and they revived my heart. That was the beginning of a change for the better. A love-elixir that warmed the blood again. I thank you, I thank everyone for it. It sustained me through all those days. If I arrive safely tomorrow (Saturday), then I will first go to my hotel, but of course it is not possible [for you] to write to that address. Ten days to get there, ten days for your reply letter. I can write back again on September 17 at the very earliest. So write to *Messrs.' J. Kennedy Tod and Co, 45 Wall Street, New York.*[3] I will leave instructions there. From there I will leave for the Adirondack Mountains to stay there for 4 weeks. I need it. Luckily my throat is better, and the fistula[4] also held up well. So I can give praise and am in good spirits. And yet I feel the separation. *Ten days* removed from one another tells upon the heart. On August 31 I will send a telegram to the Queen.[5] I hope to hear a lot of

---

1   Sugared lemon juice.

2   Guillaume (Guy) Kuyper (1878–1941), Kuyper's seventh child and second youngest son. He was a military man and appointed mayor of Stedum in 1932. It is not clear which misfortune had befallen Guy.

3   Banking firm, which also invested in the mid-west of the United States.

4   Kuyper had a sore in his mouth.

5   On 31 August 1898—her eighteenth birthday—Queen Wilhelmina (1880–1962) assumed office by proclamation. On 6 September 1898 she was sworn in as queen in a joint session of the States General in the Nieuwe Kerk in Amsterdam. Although Kuyper had indicated that he would not be able to attend the inauguration, in October 1897 he had been elected as chairman of the committee that, on behalf of the Dutch Association of Journalists, would receive the approximately 160 foreign journalists attending this ceremony.

good news from home. Don't let the children shortchange me. My heart needs some love in this loneliness. May the Lord be our Protector. Goodbye my darling, kiss everyone on behalf of the husband and father who loves you so.

THE CUNARD LINE R.M.S. ''CAMPANIA'' & ''LUCANIA'' 12,950 TONS.

[3]

New York, Fifth Avenue Hotel, Madison Square
1 September 1898

My dear ones,

I have been in New York[1] for five days now, and tomorrow I leave for the Adirondack Mountains. So first a letter. I can barely manage, because, just imagine, it's 100 degrees Fahrenheit here. For me, with my weak constitution, almost unbearable. Everything else is well-appointed. A bathroom adjoins my room and ice water is served in a jug at regular intervals. But what weighs heavily is that the evening does not bring relief. Last night I waited until one o'clock, and then it was still 93 [degrees]. For two hours I took refuge on a "roof garden," a garden on top of a roof, seven stories high, and there was one spot where every ten minutes there was a light breeze, and so there we stood with a small group of people waiting for it, and enjoying it for a moment. Apart from that, 3 collars a day, endless handkerchiefs, and everyone a fan. No insects, fortunately. The food here is nothing special. All kinds of strange dishes that don't taste good to me. Chicken leathery and dry. Everything without exception is expensive here. A carriage from the boat to the hotel ƒ7.50. An ordinary summer hat, in Amsterdam at most ƒ5, is here $5 = ƒ12.50.[2] And so everything is proportionately expensive.

What was very nice when arriving at the pier was seeing the American warships from San Jago, such as the Brooklyn, the

---

1 Kuyper stayed at the Fifth Avenue Hotel, opened in 1858. It was the first hotel in the United States to have elevators, "vertical railway cars," and an "elegant dining salon where powerful politicians held court, and where Theodore Roosevelt advanced his career in the 1880s." Cf. Marcia Reiss, *New York Then and Now*, rev. ed. (San Diego, 2005), 76.

2 The US dollar exchange rate for one Dutch guilder/*gulden* (florin = ƒ) at the time was about 40¢.

Teka, the New York, etc., a fleet of 15 ships. On Monday I also saw the return of the 71st regiment from San Jago.[3] 330 of the 1,080 men, all the others killed, wounded or ill. And even of those 330, there were a whole lot who had to ride in horse carts. Most interesting otherwise. At least 400,000 people, all wild with enthusiasm. Everything was perfectly organized. Road sweepers in front, a tidy body of men in blue-and-white uniforms, with white hats, surrounding a beautiful red iron cart with two neatly harnessed horses, to pick up the dung.[4] Then lines of policemen, three rows deep. All gentlemen, without insignias or anything of that sort, but with white pith helmets, cloaks of blue linen draping the shoulders,[5] and white gloves. Behind them the mounted police, in similar dress. Then the bands, etc. The troops looked exhausted and weak. A chaplain led the way, and when they had arrived all heads were bared, and in the open air a prayer of gratitude [was said].[6] So very different than in our country. That is the aftereffect of Calvinism. The whole of life here meets my expectations entirely. Far more than in Europe. Under everything a higher foundation. Precious as gold, in my eyes. And then *no paupers*.[7] Only well-dressed people. A laborer earns ƒ7.50 a day, that is ƒ2,250 per annum.

Fortunately, I have not been bothered by reporters. They have taken no notice whatsoever of my arrival. I was only listed in a daily paper as one of the new guests of this hotel, and that resulted in a visit by a seedy-looking Dutchman who asked me for 50 dollars. The Rev. De Vries[8] of Princeton, who translated

---

3 During the Spanish-American War of April–August 1898, the United States captured San Jago (Santiago de Cuba), along with the whole of the island. Cuba was then established as an independent state under American supervision.

4 Cf. Kuyper, *Varia Americana* (Amsterdam, 1899), 48.

5 A wide cloak that was draped around the shoulders and fastened with a cord.

6 Cf. Kuyper, *Varia Americana*, 21.

7 Ibid, 1–3; see also letter 9.

8 John Hendrik de Vries (1859–1939), pastor of the Second Presbyterian

my *Encyclopaedie*,[9] is the only one who came to visit me, and [he] told me that the publication of the *Encyclopaedie* had become possible because of an old lady[10] who had given *f*3,000 for it. The publisher would not have done it otherwise. This to make you understand that there is not much enthusiasm here [for my work]. Everything all of you imagined is incorrect. Things are, as I always said it would be, perfectly quiet, and this suits

Professor Geerhardus Vos

Church in Princeton, New Jersey (1897-1905). De Vries was a Dutchman who had emigrated from the Netherlands and from 1892 on translated much of Kuyper's work for the American market. John Hendrik should not be confused with his brother Henri de Vries (1847–1932), who translated Kuyper's *The Work of the Holy Spirit* (New York, 1900).

9 A. Kuyper, *Encyclopaedie der heilige godgeleerdheid*, 3 vols. (Amsterdam, 1893/94). From the very beginning Kuyper had an English translation of his *Encyclopaedie* in mind. The translation of the *Encyclopaedie* was first undertaken by American theologians of Dutch descent, who all had to cease this time-consuming work owing to their appointments as professors. Involved were Geerhardus Vos (1862–1949), who shortly after starting the translation in 1893 had to give it up because of his appointment as professor at Princeton Theological Seminary; subsequently Abel Henry Huizinga (1859–1905), minister of the Reformed Church in New Paltz (1886–1894), who in 1894 translated the first hundred pages or so, but who had to stop the work owing to his appointment as a professor at McCormick Theological Seminary in Chicago; and Jacob Poppen (1858–1920), who in 1896 almost completed the first volume, but then had to give up translating because of his appointment as a professor at the Meiji Gakuin Seminary in Tokyo. Vos had been asked by Kuyper, the other two by B. B. Warfield. The translation that finally appeared in print was that of De Vries and included the beginning of the first, introductory volume and the entire second, general volume of the three-volume *Encyclopaedie*. This edition, which included a foreword by Kuyper, an introduction by Warfield, and a note by De Vries, was published by Charles Scribner's Sons of New York in 1898. Eerdmans of Grand Rapids brought out a reprint in 1954 under the title *Principles of Sacred Theology*.

10 Not traced.

ENCYCLOPEDIA

OF

SACRED THEOLOGY

ITS PRINCIPLES

BY

ABRAHAM KUYPER, D.D.
FREE UNIVERSITY, AMSTERDAM

TRANSLATED FROM THE DUTCH
BY REV. J. HENDRIK DE VRIES, M.A.

WITH AN INTRODUCTION BY
PROFESSOR BENJAMIN B. WARFIELD, D.D., LL.D.
OF PRINCETON THEOLOGICAL SEMINARY

NEW YORK
CHARLES SCRIBNER'S SONS
1898

Encyclopedia of Sacred Theology

In New York, Rev. John de Vries presented Kuyper with a copy of Kuyper's recently published *Encyclopedia of Sacred Theology*.

me fine. Yesterday I went to Spring Lake Beach to visit Dr. De Witt[11] of Princeton. A seaside resort, but not as in Scheveningen, with practically no beach. His wife was the first female creature that I talked to since leaving Liverpool. I like the type. Not a trace of the coquette. Free in her movements and ready for conversation.[12] Today I looked in for a moment on cousin Broes van Heekeren[13] at his office. Ellis[14] is in the country. He sat there in a tiny little cubby-hole in dingy neighborhood. To feel sorry

---

11 John de Witt (1842–1923), professor of church history at Princeton Theological Seminary (1892–1912).

12 Cf. Kuyper's opinion of American women in *Varia Americana*, 38–40.

13 J. Broes van Heekeren, who had immigrated to America, was a son of Willem Broes van Heekeren and Hendrika Petronella Schaay, Mrs. Kuyper's eldest sister.

14 Ellis Broes van Heekeren, the wife of J. Broes van Heekeren (see previous note).

for. Kennedy Tod and Co, 45 Wall Street, were very kind and friendly. For the present send everything there, then I will get it in due course. Yesterday I sent a telegram to the Queen, which cost me ƒ68, but I had to do it now.[15] This morning I received a thank-you note in reply. As for preaching, up till now I have only heard a lady in the street. Very interesting. She arrived on a bicycle with a neatly dressed girl of 10, also on a bike. Herself all in black with a straw hat. Got off. Baby stood there with the two bicycles like a little flower, and she began. Beautiful voice, melodious English, calm, peaceful. But no substance. Against the churches and the ministers. None of that was necessary. Only Jesus, and then some vague commonplaces. And yet I was struck by the simplicity, the courage, and the fearlessness with which she carried it off.

While out walking I lost a tooth, but it has been beautifully put back in, and my wound was cleaned with a steam-driven pump and afterwards I literally did not notice it any more. How wonderful. Not expensive either. New tooth and everything, all for ƒ15. My throat too is all better, and I feel fine. The beauty of life here is: strength through self-confidence, which gives a person inner peace. Things are arranged much better than in Europe. Everything is colossal in size. Houses with 16 stories in abundance. And yet peaceful, far more than in Paris or London. Everything is also healthier and more ethical. There is also vice of course, but [it is] more latent. The aspect of life is purer.

And tomorrow up the Hudson to Albany by boat, and from there up into the mountains. I am looking forward to it. You are probably all in the midst of much activity. Don't let dear mother

15 On 31 August 1898 Kuyper sent a telegram to Queen Wilhelmina from New York, the text of which was included in English in *De Standaard*, 13 September 1898: "To Her Majesty the Queen of the Netherlands. On the day of Her Majesty's enthronement I beg most respectfully to tender My Most Gracious Queen my allegiance as a loyal subject and my entire concurrence with the forthcoming swearing in of the States General. May Her Majesty's reign be long and prosperous, and may God bless it to Her Majesty's happiness, to the welfare of the Netherland commonwealth and to the glory of His name. Dr. A. Kuyper, Member of the States General."

overexert herself too much. In my thoughts I am always with you. Do not forget me either. Goodbye dearest mama, goodbye dear children. Live together in sweet harmony. Give my regards to all the friends. I commend you to our faithful God and Father. Your most loving husband and father.

[4]

United States Hotel, Saratoga Springs
4 September 1898

My dear ones,

I have toiled through truly anxious days, and still the heat has not passed. In New York temperatures have been as high as 107 degrees, and according to the papers it's never lasted this long. Read what it says in the daily papers that I am sending you, and see what I have suffered. Soldiers who endured the heat lying outside San Jago, Cuba, collapsed here and died. Every day a long list of victims. And then me with my full-blooded constitution. You can imagine what I went through. It was unbearable. No relief anywhere. Not a sigh, not a breeze. The best thing to do was to lie down on the floor with next to nothing on. And that continued for nights and days. Even on the Hudson boat a person succumbed. Much worse than we had in Cologne that time. In Albany the same thing. The first time that it improved somewhat was here in Saratoga where the thermometer reached 94 degrees. To be sure, now and again there is a thunderstorm, but oddly, a thunderstorm without a breath of wind, nor a leaf turning nor a drop of rain falling, and it remains as warm as it was. Repeatedly I felt that I was in danger. My head felt as if held in a vise. I hardly dared move for fear of injuring myself. Ice water is the only thing that offers any relief, and throughout New York City ice is distributed free of charge; all day long ambulances drive around and pedestrians are helped onto trolley-cars to get them off the streets. I had been so afraid of it but hoped that the heat would pass, as did the newspapers, who claimed that something like this had never been endured in September before. I nearly did not succeed in packing my trunks.

And yet I managed to leave. And the Hudson is beautiful, four times the width of the Rhine, hilly banks, crystal clear water, and boats like palaces. Everything here was founded by the Dutch. Albany too. A Dutch shipmaster was the first to sail up the Hudson.[1] A small house here, made of stone from Boskoop, the first house to be built from stone, had to be demolished recently and the stone has been preserved as a monument. Still, I did not go to see anything in Albany, but remained quietly at home. I cannot bear to wear clothes. Within minutes everything was wet and unusable. I couldn't wear collars. Here in Saratoga I can finally catch my breath again. My hotel has 2,000 rooms. I have no. 666, very low.[2] The dining-hall is monstrously large, and all the waiters are blacks. Very polite. Only a few ladies made use of the heat to reveal anything, but not even 3 in a hundred, and then still very much *comme il faut* [as it should be]. Everything here is so proper. The women [are] truly more simple and solid than in Europe. You see nothing here of that vulgarity. Nor of drinking. Water and squash is all one sees. Saratoga is a

---

1 In 1609, flying the flag of the United East India Company, a Dutch trading company, the English navigator Henry Hudson sailed his ship the *Halve Maen* up the river that would later be named after him.

2 Cf. the description of American hotels in Kuyper, *Varia Americana*, 37f: "Adjoining your bedroom you can get your own bathroom with lavatory. In every room there is a washbasin with cold and warm water. For a price that is not too high you can sign up for all the meals, often numbering no less than five: 'early breakfast,' full breakfast, luncheon, dinner and supper. And all this is so sumptuous that the menu is repeatedly overloaded, serving oysters twice a day and with every midday meal sorbet as well as ice cream. In addition, the halls have been arranged in such a splendid and practical way that in the lobby of every large hotel you can find typewriters, a telegraph, postal services, a bookstore, a tobacconist, a livery office and telephone, and several wide elevators that go up and down without interruption. Add to this that the 'porter' you invariably have to report to in our country does not exist over here, but that you always find a broad desk with several 'gentlemen' behind it who are prepared to give you information—and you will understand how lengthy journeys have ceased to be a plague in America and have become, rather, a luxury, thanks to an abundance of comfort."

kind of Interlaken, but with very low mountains. Everywhere medicinal springs, neatly appointed. Take a look at the enclosed newspaper article "New Calvinism," a surprise from Dr. Horne.[3] Keep this (as well as those articles about the heat) and mention it to Rutgers.[4] I enjoyed reading it. That Dr. Horne: just like a second little me. To make one shout for joy. Who knows what the Lord has in store.

Tomorrow I am going to the Adirondacks. They lie to the north near Canada, just under Montreal and Quebec. And yet I do not have an address to pass on, because there are only endless hotels and "camps" there. Please keep sending the letters to Kennedy Tod and Co, 45 Wall Street. "Camps" are parties of 100 people or more who bring tents and spend their holidays in the mountains and forests. Transportation is by way of the lakes. Cheap, but an outing. Typically the kind of thing Rutgers loves to organize.

I will see what it's like in the mountains. I'm afraid it may be disappointing because of the lowness, the highest just 1,000 meters, and all the hotels at 200 meters at most, lower [than] in Innsbruck. But there is nothing else.[5] The high mountains lie 4 days and nights away by train, and I don't dare to [travel there] in such heat. The food here is even poorer than in New York. Cooked shellfish (clams) is the favorite dish here. Clam soup, clams in the shell, boiled, baked, grilled clams and crabs. No vegetables. Meat so so. Melons (cantaloupes) delicious. Every morning at breakfast another whole one. And now my little sheet of paper is full again. All of you up to your necks in celebrations.[6] May everything come to a good end. Give my Kennedy address

---

3   C. Silvester Horne's article was published in Dutch under the title "Een verjongd calvinisme" in *De Heraut* of 1 January 1899.

4   Frederik Lodewijk Rutgers (1836–1917), professor of church history and church law at the Vrije Universiteit in Amsterdam (1880–1910) and Kuyper's friend.

5   Kuyper was an amateur mountain climber and often visited the Alps.

6   The celebrations referred to were those held in Amsterdam on the occasion of the swearing-in of Queen Wilhelmina.

to Deen,[7] and if you [see] the gentlemen, give them my best regards. Do likewise to the brothers and accept for yourself, my dearest wife and dear children, a heartfelt handshake and a kiss from your very warm father.

---

7 Jacques Deen, editor of the *Deli-Courant*, was the treasurer of the Dutch Association of Journalists (1897–1902) and a member of the committee responsible for receiving the foreign journalists who attended Queen Wilhelmina's swearing-in ceremony; see letter 2 note 5 (2:5). On 18 August 1898 Kuyper wrote a letter in French from Hotel Cecil in London to the foreign journalists in which he apologized for his absence.

[5]

St. Hubert's Inn, Keene Heights

10 September 1898

My dear ones,

That was quite a disappointment this week, not to hear anything from home! Don't do that, I am so alone. Your letters were dated August 18. If you had written again a week later, August 25, I would have had the most recent news. Thanks to Charles'[1] good offices I have already received the *Handelsblad*[2] of August 31. My address is and remains Messrs.' J. Kennedy Tod and Co, 45 Wall Street, New York. I cannot give another address. Sending and receiving separate us by 20 days. So never write to another address, because then letters will go missing. And from New York I can receive them where I am staying within a day.

Things are going well for me here. I am in Keene Valley, something like Zell am See. Surrounded by mountains and lakes. A good hotel. Beautiful walks in wild woods. Wonderful fresh mountain air, but so cold that we have already stoked a good fire. Imagine the transition. A week ago suffocating in the heat, and now next to a large fire. Thankfully I am coming round. I still cannot sleep very well. Bad dreams all the time, then suddenly waking up and unable to get back to sleep again. Proof that the mountain air stimulates and improves the blood, and for that very reason makes one's system restless. The people here are not in the least sociable. Almost nobody talks to me, and I usually

---

1 Charles Boissevain (1842–1927), editor-in-chief of the *Algemeen Handelsblad* (1896–1908) and chairman of the Dutch Association of Journalists (1895–1899).

2 *Algemeen Handelsblad*, a Liberal newspaper published in Amsterdam since 1828.

spend my days walking or climbing alone. Climbing is difficult here. The roads are atrocious. Once I made a bad fall and tore everything to shreds, with a wind in my back, but it ended all right. I don't notice much of the ladies here. There is one sitting next to me at table who cackles away in a general American-English manner, but of conversation not a trace. I have a good room this time with an enormous table in it, on which I have spread out all my work, and now I am going to try to shorten my lectures[3] and write a speech for Hartford.[4] The weather is holding out superbly. A cool breeze, clear skies and a beautiful starry sky in the evening. Then I see the same stars that you see at home, and that brings me closer to you. That is when I feel at home again.

I am taking this time in order to recuperate. I was as exhausted as I have ever been, and the heat gave the final push. By telegraph the papers here gave good reports of the celebrations so that I was able to follow everything. It seems that all went well, for which I am deeply grateful. I feel so sorry for that young little queen. It is so overly much for a child of 18. Write to me at length about which celebrations you took part in. I saw that the trustees and curators were also invited to the Nieuwe Kerk.[5] A daily paper here showed a photograph of the church, but by mistake printed a photograph of the new Roman Catholic church opposite the railway station instead.[6] How time flies! I will be back before you realize it. Before I receive an answer to this letter I will already be in Princeton. I am thinking of staying here for

---

3   Before his departure to the United States, Kuyper had finished his first draft in English of the six Stone Lectures he was to deliver at Princeton Theological Seminary.

4   Hartford Theological Seminary, Congregationalist seminary in Hartford, Connecticut, founded in 1833.

5   Queen Wilhelmina's swearing-in ceremony took place in the Nieuwe Kerk in Amsterdam. The administrators of the Vrije Universiteit—trustees and curators—attended the ceremony.

6   The Roman Catholic Sint Nicolaaskerk, consecrated in 1887, is situated kitty-corner from Central Station.

another fourteen days, and then go to Niagara. My mouth is still doing excellently. I don't notice it any more. Our host here is a member of the church of Rev. Griffis[7] who visited us recently. And now, dear wife and dear children, I commend you to our faithful God and Father. Don't forget again to write every week. For everyone a kiss in thoughts from your most loving husband and father.

St. Hubert's Inn as depicted on its stationary.

---

7   William Elliot Griffis (1843–1928), American Congregationalist minister and publicist who wrote in particular about Japan and the Netherlands. He traveled to the Netherlands ten times and attended Queen Wilhelmina's inauguration. Griffis had known Kuyper since 1891 and had visited him at home several times. He also visited the family during the inaugural celebrations.

[6]

My dear wife and children,

It is now September 17, in two days' time exactly a month ago that I boarded ship, and still I have not received a word from home while in America. Yet if you had written every week I should have had three letters by now. Really, that is not nice, and hurts me doubly now that I am here, so far away, alone in the mountains, and all the more because I don't know your address on White[1] and so must send this letter by way of Amsterdam. However, all my complaining does not help. I must wait patiently. I am still here in this peaceful little town, and luckily have only fine weather. This week I have taken to hand one lecture a [day] to shorten it, so now they have all been reduced to 34 pages each. I have had to work hard on them. Sometimes from 9 to 4 o'clock. But now I have finished, that at least gives me peace.

However, now all kinds of other business looms. From Paterson, from Cleveland, from Hartford, from New Brunswick, from Sioux Center, from Pella, from Grand Rapids, from everywhere I receive letters inviting me to come and lecture. In that respect my rest is over. They do not know where I am of course, but they write to Princeton, and from there the letters are sent on to me. I don't know how much of all this I will be able to do. October 23[2] is Princeton's Foundation Day. Then I will have to be there for the doctorate. Thus I will not be able to travel to the west before that time. If I want to arrive back in Amsterdam be-

---

1   Kuyper meant the Isle of Wight off the south coast of England, where his wife and three daughters were staying from mid-September.

2   The correct date of Princeton's Founding Day is October 22.

tween November 10 and 12, I will have to be back in New York by November 1, and in the one week, between [October] 23 – November 1, not all that much can be accomplished. From New York to Chicago by train already takes 30 hours there and 30 hours back. From there to Sioux Center an additional 16 hours there and 16 hours back. It is actually too great an undertaking. In addition to that, they all want not only a lecture, but also a banquet, so you have to stay at each place for two days. Improvising will be the best thing to do. I don't have the time to write lectures. In New Brunswick and Philadelphia on the other hand the societies are English, so I cannot improvise there.

Thankfully I am making good progress with my constitution, gaining strength and feeling healthy, and my life here has become less lonely too. I now sit at table with a Rev. Benson[3] and his wife, who are very friendly. I was invited to dine at a few cottages, and then had a nice evening. Other guests have become more friendly too. I also get along better with the food, so that my stay here is really pleasant, also because of a better room with a cupola and three windows on the first floor. See blue line on drawing.[4] Even the animal world takes pity on me, and when I climb a mountain alone, the hotel's dog, a beautiful large purebred, faithfully accompanies me; but thinks I walk too fast, and then lies down right in front of me on the narrow path, as if to say: Try and get past me now! I received the *Standaard* and the *Handelsblad* again, so that I am once more somewhat abreast of things. Just as well that I, tired as I was, did not experience those exhausting 14 days of celebrations. If I had had to go to America in a hurry afterwards, and then immediately get ready to pitch in over here, it would quite simply not have worked. I think I will stay here for another 14 days of peace in order to regain my strength, and then may the Lord give me strength for

---

3 Louis Fitzgerald Benson (1855–1930), Presbyterian minister, editor of the *Journal of the Presbyterian Historical Society* in Philadelphia.

4 Kuyper wrote on St. Hubert's Inn stationery, which had a picture of the hotel in the letterhead. With a line on the picture he indicated which hotel room was his.

this far-from-easy task. The language here is difficult. When they talk busily among themselves, I quite simply cannot understand a word of it, especially not of the lower classes. And yet this is gradually improving somewhat, so that I hope I won't feel too intimidated when performing in Princeton. Luckily things are not expensive here. I can get by on ƒ10 a day. That will truly help me through the month. The cold has now gone, summer is back, and I am sitting before an open window writing in my flannels. I do hope you are having a good time on Wight, and that you forward[5] my letters from there to Bram and Guy and Herman.[6] For the rest, I will remain cross until a letter arrives, and from now on I count on regular letters every week. Goodbye dear wife, goodbye dear children. A heartfelt embrace from your most loving husband and father.

---

5 Comments by Mrs. Kuyper in the margin of the letter: "After [leaving] this place I wrote him a letter immediately upon my return. Please send this letter to Aunt Anna, and I hereby inform her also that we have already sent 5 letters to the address we received from father." Aunt Anna was Anna Christina Elisabeth Mond nee Kuyper (1834–1920), Kuyper's eldest sister.

6 Herman Huber (Her) Kuyper (1864–1945), Kuyper's first child. He was pastor of the Reformed Church of Leeuwarden (1896–1899) and from 1900 professor of church history and church polity at the Vrije Universiteit in Amsterdam.

[7]

St. Hubert's Inn, Keene Heights
24 September 1898

My dear wife,

Another week has passed, and yesterday I finally received your letter, which had been posted in Amsterdam on September 10. I have been without a word from home from August 20 until September 23, whereas if one letter had been written every week I could have had and should have had three letters by now. As it is, from August 18 until September 10, that is 23 days or more than 3 weeks, no mail for me from Amsterdam. And to console me you now add that the next letter will come from Ventnor,[1] which will not be sent before September 19 or 20. Thus that one I will receive around October 4. Now I quite understand that amid the celebrations everything was topsy-turvy and there was no moment of peace, but surely a postcard could not have been too much of an effort, especially as all five of you were at home. I wrote every 7 days. If you knew what it is like to hear nothing from your dear wife and children for more than a month, at such a distance, you would understand that I miss something here that I would rather not have missed.

I am truly glad that you enjoyed the celebrations so much and that I was able to get you admitted everywhere, thanks to my position.[2] Deen is a dear man. Warm-hearted and appreciative, but I had not expected him to be otherwise. Boissevain[3] regularly sent me the *Handelsblad*, and the papers here were also

---

7 Victorian seaside resort on the Isle of Wight where Kuyper's wife and daughters stayed for a few weeks in September and October 1898.

8 See note 4:6.

9 See note 5:1.

25

very informative. In other words, I am fully informed and closely followed events at home. It pains me, not so much that other people but that even you seem to doubt the sincerity of what I wrote in *De Standaard*.[4] What they demanded from me was simply impossible. If I had had to carry on working until after the celebrations in Amsterdam [on] all those special editions, and be in charge of those journalists until September 17, I would have succumbed. You have no idea how dead tired I was and how that mouth affair had weakened me further. Usually I go on holidays by the first of July. This time it was five weeks later, August 11. But if another 5 weeks had been added, and then weeks such as they were, and if I had had to go at it at once here in America, Jo, then I would have collapsed. That was not permissible. My task and mission in life are too serious for that. Here too, work and the pressure of activities are never far away. I was not able to avoid having to add another lecture, in English, this time without assistance; and apart from that they want me to give speeches and appear in public everywhere, all the way to the West, in Iowa, which is three days by train from here. Even Dosker[5] wrote to me: Be sure to stay calm, brace yourself, because the bustle that awaits you could otherwise have grave consequences. I am not here for pleasure. I am here to try and introduce the truth I cherish with all my soul and see it find acceptance here as well. And all sorts of friends here hope exactly that of my visit. But the difficulties are unbelievable. The decline here was considerable, and without anyone realizing it. And yet I hope to persevere; but to think that I might have gone through all that in Amsterdam

---

1 In *De Standaard* of 1 September 1898 Kuyper wrote an asterism entitled "De regeering aanvaard" (Acceded to the throne). The gist of this short editorial was that it was a blessing that there was still a bond between the Netherlands and the house of Orange.

2 Henry Elias Dosker (1855–1926), professor of historical theology at Western Theological Seminary, the western seminary of the Reformed Church in America located in Holland, Michigan. Dosker was a Dutchman who had immigrated to the United States in 1873 with his parents. He came from Secessionist (1834) circles and made Kuyper more widely known in the United States.

first, then work myself to the bone here, and then arrive home and face everything in Amsterdam again: it does not take into account my finite strength. Don't forget, I will soon be 61 years old.

Right now we are having rain and wind and fog, so I think I will leave for Boston and Hartford this Wednesday or Thursday and travel from there to New York on Saturday. They asked me to preach in English there, but I don't think I will. On Monday and Tuesday I am going to Princeton to meet the gentlemen, and to seek help from a dentist for my mouth, which has not been doing so well again these last three days. It must be the weather. I will probably lecture in Princeton on the 8th, 9th, 12th, 18th, 19th and 20th [of October]. In between [I speak] in Paterson and Philadelphia (in the Historical Presbyterian Society[6]), on the 22nd receive the doctor's diploma, and on the 24th and 26th lecture in Hartford and New Brunswick.[7] After that I go to Chicago, where I have to deliver a speech in the Holland Society.[8] Then on to Grand Rapids and Holland, Michigan. And from there I have to go to Cleveland, Pella, Orange City, no doubt to return completely exhausted. I will probably sail back on the boat that leaves on Tuesday November 15. The previous one leaves on November 5, but I don't think I'll manage to be ready by then. But more about that later. A peek into my program will be enough to convince you that indeed I do not face a sinecure here. Enjoy Ventnor to the full, and kiss my dear girls for me. May you and they be commended to God by your loving husband.

---

3   The Presbyterian Historical Society in Philadelphia, founded in 1852, has a library and archival material that has a bearing on the history of the Presbyterian Church in the United States. See also note 6:3.

4   The theological school of the Dutch Reformed Church in New Brunswick, in New Jersey, founded in 1784. This was/is the oldest seminary in the United States.

5   The Holland Society or Nederlandsche Vereeniging in Chicago, founded in 1895, was a social club for Americans who cherished their Dutch origins; it numbered approximately eighty members.

[8]

The Brunswick, Back Bay, Boston
1 October 1898

Dear wife and children,

It is now almost one and a half months ago that I received the collection of letters in Liverpool, and in all that time I have not received anything at all, except one short letter from mother. I will not speak of it anymore. Answer the question for yourselves whether it is all right, or in accordance with the demands of love. On Wednesday I left Keene Valley and at night slept in Elizabethtown. From there by coach and train to Boston. In all, a journey of 11 hours. The distances here are enough to scare you. Looking at a map you'd think that Boston was near New York. And yet it will take me eight hours by train to get there this evening, while traveling faster than to The Hague. It is muggy and stiflingly warm again, puzzling for this time of year.

Boston is the rich city of America; as a result, the opulence here exceeds everything and everything is proportionately expensive. When I gave the shoeshine boy 12½ cents for polishing my shoes once, he refused; according to the rates for polishing shoes, he is to get 25 cents each time. And it's the same with everything. My laundry bill for some socks, collars, handkerchiefs always runs up to ƒ4. But what impressed me here even more than in New York is the general decency and decorum. What we call pubs do not exist. Along entire streets there is not a single café to be found, and where there are cafés they serve mostly squash and beer. One does not see "girls" in the streets. At table, wine is not drunk. People are level-headed and sober. Nor is the fair sex overly forward. They are candid and go their own way, but without giving offence or behaving improperly. In general, more respectable than our ladies. Here there is more seriousness in the population. I do not like people's taste here, nor their movements or manners. The taste is not showy but it is impure, a mixture of French and English. Nothing of the dignified air of English women or the elegance of the French. In everything one senses that the Christian religion, much more than in our country, is a source of strength. The well-to-do in particular are religious, a bit vague, but steadfast nevertheless, and to churches and schools they donate sums of money nobody would dream of in our country. That is why the magnificent buildings of the universities and the museums are incredible, and the salaries are in proportion. Professors of my [rank] have an income of ƒ20 to 25,000. Even the Roman Catholics are much better here. In Brooklyn for example they have founded a Holy Name Society[1] against profanity and have held a procession with banners in which 10,000 men participated: "Don't use in vain the name of the Lord." In our country the Roman Catholics don't care in the least about swearing.[2] Thus Protestants and Roman Catholics work together in a whole range of activities. A curse in this country are the sects. They shoot up like mushrooms. Just recently another one, which claims that our Savior returned to earth in November 1874 and is in hiding somewhere.

The requests for lectures keep coming. I'm quite at a loss what to do, and the people are so persistent. I'm afraid that it will tire me so. They all write about audiences of 4,000 people, that is 2½ times a full Keizersgracht Kerk.[3] That is why I'm afraid I will *have* to stay here until mid-November, and that I won't make it back before the end of November. Those long distances by train are my undoing. Orange City in Iowa, the farthest point I have to

1 The Holy Name Society in New York, founded in 1882, is a society of the Roman Catholic Church that holds annual processions in honor of God's name and to combat its being used in vain.

2 Cf. Kuyper, *Varia Americana*, 124–25.

3 The Keizersgracht Kerk was the first church building erected in Amsterdam by the followers of the Doleantie. The church was first used in 1888 and seated 1600 people.

be, is more than 40 hours by train from here. Luckily one can rent private compartments with sleeping accommodation. That does cost a lot, but then at least it's bearable. The railway system here has, quite simply, been beautifully designed. So robust, so trim and so spacious. Without extras, traveling by train costs ƒ3 to ƒ4 an hour. So a return journey to Orange City 2 x 4 x 40 = ƒ320. To which an extra ƒ100 is added for sleeping quarters. Except for the ticket inspectors there are black menial workers everywhere to look after you. Kind, cordial boys, happy with a "Good evening." Today I will go to Hartford, where Professor Jacobus[4] asked me to lecture. I am going to arrange it with him today. He too is most persistent. He sent me no less than 4 telegrams, to stay over for a night and to attend a reception with the students this evening. But I declined. I need my rest for meditation and correspondence. Monday I am going to size up everything in Princeton, and make my acquaintance with the gentlemen. I think I will be back in New York by Wednesday, and the following Monday the lectures in Princeton will commence. But first I have to do something about the fistula in my mouth, which festers more again than some time ago. Such a pity! Amazing, the huge dimensions everything has over here! In Wisconsin a forest fire broke out over an area of 300 English miles, that is almost 500 kilometers, almost 10 times the distance between Amsterdam and The Hague. How truly happy I am that Deen and Van Waalwijk[5] were decorated. They more than deserve it. And now one more thing. In the one little note that I have received in a month and a half, the address for Ventnor was not even mentioned. I will just have to put on an address and hope for the best. I hope that last week's

---

4 Melanchton Williams Jacobus (1855–1937), New Testament professor at Hartford Theological Seminary (1891–1928), delivered the Stone Lectures at Princeton Theological Seminary in 1897.

5 D. A. van Waalwijk (1853–1937), journalist, director of the *Niewsblad voor Nederland* (1883–1913), secretary of the Dutch Association of Journalists (1886–1892, 1895–1897), and a member of the committee for the reception of foreign journalists on the occasion of the swearing-in of Queen Wilhelmina.

letter and this one reach you. And now, dear wife and children, remember me and wake up from your letter-writing lethargy. In my thoughts I embrace and kiss you all. Be commended to our faithful God and Father by your loving husband and father.

[9]

Fifth Avenue Hotel, Madison Square, New York
8 October 1898

My dear wife and children,

This week I received a letter from mother, one from Jo, and one from Hovy.[1] That's more like it and gives me hope that those who usually write so many letters will also remember me a bit more. This week I spent toiling and moiling. On my return it really was that same sticky, clammy hot atmosphere again, just as in Pau.[2] It was unbearable. Until 12 o'clock at night not a breeze in the air. It ended in affecting my intestines and I have been struggling with diarrhea since Tuesday. That means I eat almost nothing and try by all means to get back a normal feeling below the stomach. Yesterday I took castor oil to see if anything was there. But that did not help either. The death rate, which is 1,000 per week on average, rose to 1,965. Almost double. Thankfully the "hot wave" (as it's called here) is now over. But obviously, the cold that is now setting in will do me no good in the first few days.

On Monday and Tuesday I went to have a look in Princeton, and I liked it there. De Vries and his wife and Vos[3] and

---

1 Willem Hovy (1840–1915), brewer, chairman of the Board of Trustees of the Vrije Universiteit (1879–1896), and a friend of Kuyper.

2 In October 1894 Kuyper stayed in the town of Pau in the south of France, at the foot of the Pyrénées.

3 Geerhardus Vos (1862–1949), professor of biblical theology at Princeton Theological Seminary (1893–1932). Vos was born in Holland and had immigrated in 1881 to the United States with his parents, who came from Secessionist (1834) circles. He promoted Kuyper's name in the United States.

his wife were most cordial, and Dr. Warfield[4] was very courteous. The president of the university[5] and the president of the seminary[6] had traveled to the next station to meet me. Princeton is a beautiful little town with 1,500 students, all lodged in proper residence halls.[7] I also visited that old lady who had paid *f*3,000 for the publication of the English translation of my *Encyclopaedie.* The book has now been published and looks wonderful. Only, I am to get just one copy, and have to buy all the others at *f*25 apiece. Fancy that! The accommodation in Princeton is ideal.[8] There is also

Professor Benjamin B. Warfield

Warfield was a leading theologian and a convinced supporter of neo Calvinism. He was known as an opponent of modernism and the "revivalism" embraced by many American churches.

---

4 Benjamin Breckinridge Warfield (1851–1921), professor of didactic and polemical theology at Princeton Theological Seminary (1887–1921). Warfield was regarded as a leading Presbyterian theologian in the United States.

10 Francis Landey Patton (1843–1932), professor of ethics (1886–1913) and president (1888–1902) of Princeton University, lecturer in Theism at Princeton Theological Seminary (1888–1903).

11 Prior to 1902 Princeton Theological Seminary did not have its own president as it was affiliated with Princeton University. Kuyper was probably referring to the acting chairman of the Seminary's College of Professors, William Henry Green (1825–1900), professor of Eastern and Old Testament literature (1859–1900).

12 Cf. Kuyper, *Varia Americana*, 147–48.

13 Kuyper stayed at the Princeton Inn, opposite the university and a 10-minute walk from the seminary.

a highly regarded dentist whom I visited. He is going to make two new dentures for me, but he said there was little he could do about the fistula. He too thought it would probably take another four months before it was completely healed. The only thing that still bothers me are all those luncheons and dinners they have planned for me [in Princeton]. As you know, I don't fancy them. And since you never get anything but water, the dinners are thoroughly boring.

This week I lecture on the 10th, 11th, 14th, and next week on the 19th, 20th and 21st. Then on October 22 the granting of the doctorate in law, and in the evening the president's banquet. That is a Saturday, and late on Saturday evening I return to New York, to observe a day of rest on Sunday, and on Monday at 10 o'clock I travel to Grand Rapids, which is 25 hours by train. There I will lecture on October 26, go to Holland, Michigan on the 27th, lecture there on the 28th, and on the 29th go to Chicago. So [I will celebrate] my birthday[9] in Holland; address Rev. Prof. Henry E. Dosker, D.D., Holland, Michigan. In the week of October 30 to November 6 I will go to Pella, Orange City, and back to Chicago to lecture in all *three* places. On November 6 I go to Cleveland, Ohio, to lecture there in English. Then to Buffalo, the Niagara Falls, and so back to New York once more, to lecture in Hartford, New Brunswick, Paterson, Princeton, and Philadelphia. Finally to Baltimore and Washington, [where] President McKinley[10] expects me, and where the governor[11] and the mayor[12] of Baltimore will receive me, and then on November 19 from New York back to Holland, where I might be back home in time for Tokkie's birthday.[13] You see how busy I am, but it cannot be helped. To make some headway I have to let my-

---

1 Kuyper's birthday was on October 29.

2 William McKinley (1843–1901), president of the United States (1897–1901).

3 Lloyd Lowndes, Jr. (1845–1905), governor of Maryland (1896–1900).

4 William T. Malster (1843–1907), mayor of Baltimore (1897–1899).

13 Tokkie was the nickname of Kuyper's daughter Cato, whose birthday was on November 30.

self be heard. And now with hindsight I truly understand how impossible it would have been to round off everything here if I had not arrived here a month earlier. Everything must be determined well in advance, halls rented, etc. Otherwise it cannot be arranged.

On Sunday I was most fortunate in that the Presbyterian church just past my hotel here celebrated the Lord's Supper. Peaceful and solemn. However, I did miss our Communion Form, and [I missed] *the poor*. So strange, one never sees them in church. It's as if they don't count. [I saw] only distinguished people. Things are still expensive here. When I omitted to pay for having my shoes polished, *f*0.25 was neatly charged to my account every time. My glasses broke. New ones *f*9.50. And so it is with everything. A carriage from the railway to one's hotel *f*7.50. A pair of glacé gloves *f*6.25.[14] You cannot imagine the prices. Write to me and tell me whether Fred[15] as already sent the *f*2,000. I will wait before asking him, and wrote him as much from here. On the train I had a short conversation with a black lady for the first time. You have no idea how polite and respectable they are, fine manners and a voice, half singing, as if they have a little bird in their throats. But apart from that, poor taste in clothing, jewelry, and gold. From *Del*[16] a letter [inviting me] to come and stay, which I declined. One visit depresses me enough. I am a bit scared of the West. All those Hollanders want to see me and shake hands. I hope I may be a blessing to them, and permanently reestablish the bonds. There I will find my friends Beuker[17]

---

14 These were gloves of French make. American gloves of the same quality cost *f*2.50. Cf. Kuyper, *Varia Americana*, 28.

15 Jan Frederik Hendrik (Fred, Fredy) Kuyper (1866–1933), Kuyper's second child and second-eldest son. He was a dentist in Semarang in the Dutch East Indies.

16 Not traced.

17 Henricus Beuker (1834–1900), professor of systematic and practical theology at the Theological School of the Christian Reformed Church in Grand Rapids (1894–1900). Beuker came from Secessionist (1834)

and Ten Hoor,[18] both very nice [to me] now.

Just continue to write to the old address, except for the letters before October 29, which have to be posted 13 days in advance. But no, I see now that that is pure folly. You won't get this letter before October 18 and then it's too late. So just [send] everything to the old address. That is safest. And now, my darlings, have an enjoyable time. Goodbye sweet wife. Goodbye dear children. Your loving husband and father.

circles, had been a critic of Kuyper, and had immigrated to the United States in 1893.

18 Foppe Martin ten Hoor (1855–1934), minister of the Oakdale Park Christian Reformed Church in Grand Rapids (1896–1900). Ten Hoor came from Secessionist (1834) circles, had been a relentless critic of Kuyper, and had immigrated to the United States in 1896.

[10]

Princeton
14 October 1898

My dear ones,

I presume that this letter will end up in Ventnor, and otherwise the postal services will send it on. It's a pity you don't write to me about your plans in advance. The distance is so great, and the letters arrive so late. This week I began giving my lectures here, and delivered half of them. I dreaded the first time. To speak in a foreign language before a strange audience feels strange and one never knows in advance how it will go. Moreover, I was not well. The great heat, suddenly brought to an end by a cold spell, had completely upset my intestines. I suffered from terrible diarrhea, which has now persisted for ten days and has weakened me. But, thank God, I managed, and it went well, and even better during [lectures] 2 and 3. Only a pity my lectures, because of speaking slowly in a foreign language, became too long. Sometimes *two hours*. Tiring also. But precisely because of that, I saw all the more clearly that I had succeeded. The applause was deafening, and quite soon I was as calm there as at home behind the lectern. I am also kept busy here. Every day a dinner party, and then I have to speak all the time until late at night. But there is much love and sympathy. There are fine men here, whom I could wish we had with us, but who had never realized what the actual point was and who are now happy. At De Vries's house (the translator of my *Encyclopaedie*) they are almost too kind. He and his brother[1] continually cry out: "You are our father and our teacher and our inspirer." This evening I am going to New York again to set

---

1 See note 3:8.

up a branch of the General Dutch Alliance[2] for the whole United States. I return here on Tuesday. I will give the final three lectures on the 19th, 20th, and 21st, and Saturday is Founding Day. They are now so enthusiastic that the university has decided to make me *doctor with a hood*. I will of course bring that ornament home with me. Things are getting better all the time.

Miller Chapel at Princeton Theological Seminary

Kuyper delivered his Stone Lectures on Calvinism to enthusiastic audiences in Miller Chapel. Stressing the superiority of Calvinism as a worldview in all fields of life, in six lectures he successively discussed Calvinism as it pertained to history, religion, politics, science, art, and the future. According to the British historian Peter Heslam, the Stone Lectures offer "the most complete, cogent, and visionary expression of Kuyperian thought."

But that is not all. Requests for me to come and speak are coming in from all quarters now. [Discourses] from both a Christian and a Dutch point of view. I really don't know what to do. For example, I received an invitation from the College Women's Club in Rochester to come and lecture, and afterwards they would travel with me through the Mohawk Valley and to

---

2   See note 13:11.

the Falls of Niagara. Not just one letter, but what is known here as "an epistolary bombardment." I wish I could send you a small sample just for fun. I will certainly not leave [for Europe] before November 19, and it is by no means certain that I will succeed in doing even that. It will depend on whether I can last, speaking *day after day*, facing an audience of 4,000 after spending the night on the train. I doubt it very much, and given my sensitive constitution I have to be careful not to catch a fever. Day in day out, from morning till evening, always surrounded by people, always speaking until late at night overstimulates my brain so much. In addition, I received an invitation from Chicago to come and deliver at least 4 of the lectures[3] there. I have to speak twice there for the people from Holland. That makes *six* speaking engagements in that city alone. And yet it is so difficult to refuse. In all those faculties faithful brothers face *very weak ones*. Now that they managed to get me invited, they hope to strengthen their position. If I decline the others will rejoice. They are prepared to go to great lengths. For this work Chicago offers me *f*750 plus entertainment. I also have to go to the Dutch colonies. Those people are on the alert. One wrote to me: Every day people drop in to ask whether you are coming, and if there is just a little hope they take courage. I think I can gain entrance for *De Heraut*[4] in the future and so obtain a lasting influence. Furthermore, I cannot be in Washington for too short a time either. Not only do I have to see the President[5] but also the members of the Cabinet. So be prepared that I might return later than expected. As I will be too busy to write, you will receive my next letter somewhat later—though only seven days later at most.

I am discovering more and more that I was meant to be

---

3   Kuyper was referring to the six Stone Lectures that he was delivering at Princeton.

4   *De Heraut* (The Herald), a church weekly, of which Kuyper was editor-in-chief from 1871 till 1920.

5   Cf. telegram dated 4.10.1898 from C. W. van der Hoogt, Baltimore, to A. Kuyper, Fifth Av. Hotel, New York: "President will have returned beginning November will be pleased to receive you letter following."

here and that it was most necessary that I came. Here too the backsliding lies hidden behind a facade and is on the point of breaking through. Just imagine, in the Dutch Reformed Church in New York even ladies got up in front of the audience to sing, and when I asked what kind of ladies they were, they said: opera singers, and this was even defended here at a dinner. At table I openly stated: *I think it a shame for any Christian church.*[6] And it is exactly that decisiveness that is lacking here. They do see the danger, but remain silent. This in particular gives me a sense of mission. Just yesterday evening a retired professor said to me: "It is in the way of providence, Sir, that you came to us." And now I take my leave again, once more press you all to my heart, commend all my darlings to God, and remain in His faithfulness. Your loving husband and father.

---

6   Cf. Kuyper, *Varia Americana*, 127.

[11]

Princeton Inn, Princeton
22 October 1898

Today, dear wife and children, the time to write is short. I'm eager to start packing for New York, and I've been fully occupied until now. My days have been extremely busy. Yesterday I gave the last of the six lectures and then attended a dinner party at the president's: ladies and gentlemen in full evening dress, such as we do not see at home. So the whole evening was spent being introduced to endless ladies and gentlemen, and so I did not get home until twelve. At 9 o'clock this morning they were at my door again. It was Founding Day. I was picked up in toga, taken to a hall where the hood was put on my shoulders, and then again the introductions to all the gentlemen trustees and professors, among them former President Cleveland.[1] We all marched in procession to Alexander Hall, a beautiful building with galleries, where sat a thousand students as well as gentlemen and ladies. I had the place of honor: former President Cleveland on one side and myself on the other. Then came the presidential address, and afterwards the awarding of the doctorate. The dean read out the resolutions and documents, with a summary of the man's merits, and then the president asked if I wanted to say anything. Whereupon I gave an impromptu speech, which succeeded so well that it ended in sustained applause and the professor of oratory thanked me for that specimen of English eloquence. God enabled me, I don't know how myself, amid that placid company to speak up for God and for professing His Name. The impression

---

1   Grover Cleveland (1837–1908), twice president of the United States (1885–1889; 1893–1897). After his presidency Cleveland lived in Princeton and was a trustee of Princeton University.

41

made was amazing.[2] Afterwards everyone came to me. The Hollanders were congratulated on having such a compatriot, and all the ladies were allowed to shake hands. Well, let me thank God for it. "People were all beaming," said one lady; and I can only say, "It was a perfect day."

Do not worry about the letters anymore. I received everything all in one go. Today from Bram 8 pages. I am now going back to New York and Monday to Grand Rapids, where I will arrive on Tuesday. I speak there on Wednesday, in Holland on Thursday, will attend a banquet on Friday, and go to Chicago on Saturday. Address: Rev. R. H. Joldersma,[3] 195 Hastings Street, Chicago, Illinois. The week after that I go to Pella and Orange City, 24 hours by train, and arrive back in Chicago that Saturday, where I will stay for the week of November 6 to 13. Keep writing to Kennedy Tod and Co. That is safest. Goodbye for now, dear wife and children. Be commended to God by your loving husband and father.

---

2   Kuyper's co-laureate, the British, Oxford professor of English law, Albert Venn Dicey (1835-1922), was also impressed with Kuyper's performance. In a letter to his wife, he wrote: "We were each asked to say a few words. This led to the most remarkable speech I have heard in a long time. Kuyper . . . looked like a Dutchman of the seventeenth century. He spoke slowly and solemnly. His English was impressive, with here and there a Dutch idiom. He told us he was a Calvinist; that he had been persecuted by anti-Calvinists—this itself sounded like the language of another age. All the good in America had its root in Calvinism, which was as much a legal and an ethical as a religious creed. The Continental States had sympathized with Spain. Not so the Dutch Calvinists. 'We have not forgotten our contest with Spanish tyranny; we fought it for a hundred years. In six weeks you have given Spanish power its *coup de grace*, but neither England nor the United States would have been free but for Dutch heroism. Spain has in all countries and in all ages been a curse to the world.' . . . This was the tone of the whole speech. There was not a word of flattery to America. One felt as if the seventeenth century had visibly risen upon us to give the last curse to Spain. After that I spoke, said nothing very remarkable." See Peter S. Heslam, *Creating a Christian worldview*, 65.

3   Rense Henry Joldersma (1854–1913), pastor of the First Reformed Church in Chicago (1895–1899).

Kuyper in toga, 22 October 1898

[12]

Auditorium Hotel, Chicago
30 October 1898

After a very busy week, dear wife and children, again a word for those at home. On Monday morning (October 23[1]) I left New York and traveled by train to Detroit, where I arrived on Tuesday morning. The journey was better than I had expected. The trains on such lines are so excellently furnished that it's almost like staying in a guest house. I had my own room, with a table and a sofa. A room as big as Miss Ashton's upstairs.[2] At night it was turned into a bedroom, with a large wide bed, suitable if need be for two next to each other. For exercise you can walk through all the carriages, the length from our front door to the end of the garden. And there is a beautiful carriage that serves as a dining room, where there is ample room to sit and you can get an excellent dinner for one dollar. In my little room I had time to prepare my speech for the next day.[3]

And yet I did not sleep much. That the train stopped repeatedly and other trains passed us by, made it impossible. In Detroit I therefore took to bed for a short time. That refreshed me, and at one o'clock I went to Grand Rapids, where I arrived at six o'clock. They picked me up and had arranged an excellent hotel. Beuker led the way. Unfortunately there was carnival and it was noisy in town. In the evening I had an audience of more than 2,000 people. Wonderful, a real pleasure. All life and inspiration. *Wilhelmus* by a choir. All in all it took three hours. I was hungry.

---

4   Monday was October 24.

5   Ethel Ashton, a governess, lived in with the Kuyper family; she had helped Kuyper write his Stone Lectures in English.

6   Cf. Kuyper's description of railway carriages in *Varia Americana*, 36f.

Couldn't get anything at my hotel. The people celebrating carnival had eaten everything. Waited in a restaurant for an hour, but nothing there either. I then walked up and down the town for an hour and finally, in a backstreet, got a warm piece of meat and a cup of coffee. I slept well. At nine o'clock in the morning five landaus pulled up in front of the hotel. In them all the prominent Hollanders wearing orange[4] ribbons. And so to the high school.[5] There I had to speak in front of 900 boys and girls in English.[6] Then on to a college[7] where the students cheered and yelled. Spoke again. Back to the hotel. Eat. Again the carriages pulled up. To the station. And thus to Holland, Michigan. There 200 students to meet the train, who welcomed me with hurrahs. Of course a welcoming committee, with mayor,[8] judges, etc. Then to the hotel. In the evening a magnificent turnout. Speech.[9] Two hours. Afterwards a reception, gentlemen and ladies, at the home of Dosker.[10] Early Friday morning to Hope

---

7 Orange, owing to the House of Orange, the name of the Dutch royal family.

8 Central High School in Grand Rapids.

9 Cf. Kuyper, *Varia Americana*, 114: "When the present writer discovered to his amazement, at the high school in Grand Rapids where more than 30,000 Hollanders live, that even the girls were taught Latin, French, and German, but that Dutch was conspicuous by its absence, he let slip: *That is a shame*, by which he was not referring to the principal of the school but to the Dutch settlers who had simply neglected to use their influence at municipal elections to assert the rights of their nationality."

10 The seminary and college of the Christian Reformed Church, founded in 1876.

11 Gerben W. Mokma (1846–1912), mayor of Holland, Michigan (1898–1900).

12 In the Third Reformed Church in Holland Kuyper spoke about "Calvinism and the Future," the subject of his last Stone Lecture. Cf. Kuyper, *Varia Americana*, 93: "In conversations it became clear time and again how, for most people, English went down better. A lecture on Calvinism, delivered in Holland, Michigan, in Dutch and not in English on purpose, had, according to reliable witnesses, been understood by not even a third of the audience."

13 See note 7:5.

45

The menu card for the banquet given in Kuyper's honor on 28 October. The dishes served included "Saratoga Chips à la Kleine Luyden" and "Coquilles of Sweetbreads à la Vrije Universiteit."

College.[11] Chock-full. Gave a speech again. Then drove through Friesland, Zeeland, Drenthe, and Overijssel, all villages here. Luncheon with a farmer. Back to Holland. In the evening a large banquet at the hotel. 150 people at table. Band music. Menu

14 Hope College, founded in 1851 on the initiative of pioneer pastor A. C. van Raalte, was associated with the Reformed Church in America.

with portrait. Toasts without end. And finally spoke for half an hour. Glowing enthusiasm. Lasted until 2 o'clock tonight. Then a stand-up reception in the hall of the hotel. So strange: you have to walk past the line-up and shake two thousand hands. After the first hundred I quickly took off my ring. I couldn't stand the pain. And then they say that *many* hands make light work. Went to bed at three. Got to sleep at five. Got up at eight. Callers upon callers. Packed my bags. Wrote all kinds of letters to the English papers, which (it is election time here[12]) play me off among the parties to get the Hollanders on their side. At half past eleven lunch with the president of the Second Chamber here.[13] Traveled for an hour with Joldersma who had also come. At the train, the mayor, the gentlemen and ladies, to say farewell. Arrived in Chicago at seven o'clock. You can imagine how tired and exhausted I felt. Toward the end you are worn out. Wonderful meeting with Isaäc Verwey.[14] He has become a warm, enthusiastic Christian, has a loving wife and children. Addressed me in such a sweet way during the banquet.[15] So grateful. Many friends who had known and helped Fredy here. Numerous *Heraut* readers[16] who gave such warm thanks. It was wonderful and rich. But as I mentioned already, exhausting. While all that was going on, I wrote another article for the front page of *De Heraut*.[17] Afterwards a meditation. Now your letter. And then I am going to get

---

15 It concerned elections for the Michigan House of Representatives.

16 Probably Gerrit John Diekema (1859–1930), speaker of the Michigan House of Representatives (1889–1890).

14 Isaäc Verwey, editor of *De Grondwet* (1880–1899), a weekly newspaper published in Holland, Michigan.

15 Cf. Kuyper, *Varia Americana*, 92: "The president of the table therefore presided in a most humorous fashion in English, and except for Professor Dosker and Verwey, LL.M., and Verwey, an attorney, everyone introduced his toast in English."

16 Of the Dutch periodicals that were read in the United States at this time, *De Heraut* had the largest circulation.

17 See *De Heraut*, 13 November 1898. The front-page article bore the title "Common grace, third series, nr. LXII" and was dated "Grand Rapids, Michigan, 26 October 1898."

BE AMERICANIZED

Was Dr. Kuyper's Advice to Hollanders Here.

A MASTERLY ADDRESS

Was That Delivered at the Third Church Thursday Night.

The lecture given by Dr. Abraham Kuyper, of Amsterdam, at the Third Reformed church on Thursday evening was attended by as many persons as the spacious church would accommodate. At 7 o'clock the doors were opened and at 8 o'clock remained vacant and every available bit of space was occupied by some attentive listener.

Miss Hannah TeRoller played an organ voluntary and music was furnished by a choir consisting of Prof. J. B. Nykerk, Mrs. G. J. Diekema, Miss Kate Pfanstiehl and Dr. A. C. V. R. Gilmore.

The chairman of the evening was Prof. H. E. Dosker, of the theological seminary. After congregational singing, Rev. J. Van Houte led in prayer. Prof. J. B. Nykerk rendered an inspiring solo—"The New Jerusalem." Dr. Dosker introduced the speaker with a few well-chosen words.

Before launching out upon the discussion of his subject "The Future and Calvinism" the speaker made some pertinent remarks with regard to America and the Hollanders in it.

He said there were some words in the American language which he envied them. One of them was "whole-souled." He assured his hearers that he was in "whole-souled sympathy" with America, that he possessed much whole-souled sympathy for the Hollanders in America, and that he most heartily sympathized with the people in Holland, Michigan. In Grand Rapids he had been welcomed by the people and felt at home, but he liked Holland better as the "Dort" of America. Long before man's eye had discovered the place where Holland now stands, God had seen it and purposed to call Van Raalte here.

Another word which would express the purpose of his coming to this country, was "investigation"—which means to find God's footprints in the history of the world.

America looks forward toward a grand future but it needs the principles of Calvinism to strengthen its backbone. Too often has Calvinism been brought to the people in an unacceptable manner. Be sure and bring it with a friendly smile and offer it pure.

He believes that the future of the development of Calvinistic principles is no longer in Europe but in America. He has great love for America and at one time thought of making it his permanent home. But providence had ruled otherwise.

The bond of fellowship was strengthened by the war with Spain. As a news paper man and writer of authority he assured the people that he did his best to show the people of his country the reason for our war with Spain. At one time indeed, his was the only paper in the Netherlands upholding the policy of the United States. He was glad as a Hollander that we had whipped the Spaniards.

He rejoiced to know that the Hollanders in this country were becoming Americanized. The language of America must be yours, and the country must be your country.

Then he spoke about a certain union of Hollanders already organized in the Netherlands, in Belgium, in the Transvaal, and in the West Indies. It is called the "Dutch General Alliance" and has for its purpose the care and proper treatment and aid of Hollanders who may immigrate here, and to cause the history of the Dutch in the Netherlands and in this country to be brought more permanently before the public through our libraries and schools.

THE HOLLAND DAILY SENTINEL (or "Sentiment" as the worthy gentleman persisted in calling it) came in for its share of advertisement. The statement had been made in THE SENTINEL that the public in general would better understand and relish another subject than "Calvinism and the Future." Many were afraid that the development of that theme would bring in terms and logical reasonings beyond the grasp of the common people. Events proved the correctness of our statement.

The subject was handled in a masterly manner, and the lecture proved to be extremely learned. It was a broad survey of the history of the civilized world with a look into the future. To thoroughly grasp the subject as discussed it was necessary for one to be versed in history—profane and ecclesiastical,—in science in nearly all of its branches and in theology.

One listening to the broad survey of men and matter and deep insight into the principles underlying human affairs today, knew at once that there was a master mind. To those who could understand the lecture it was a rare treat and it will leave its impression.

This morning at ten o'clock Dr. Kuyper spoke to the students in Winant's chapel.

He did not speak on any special theme but made some general remarks about education and investigation. He asserted that Van Raalte had caught the true spirit of Calvinism when in the very earliest years of the colony he laid stress on the need of an institution for higher education.

He complimented the students on their ability to use their throats when welcoming him at the depot.

He expressed the hope that Hope College might ever remain an institution where the glory of God would be considered of supreme importance.

The chapel was filled with an appreciative audience, among the visitors being many of our citizens as well as ministers from other places.

Immediately after the lecture Dr. Kuyper was taken to a carriage, and in company with a committee consisting of Dr. , J. Kollen, Hon. Isaac Marsilje, Isaac Cappon and G. J. Van Schelven started on a drive through the surrounding farming communities. The party expects to return at about five o'clock.

This evening a reception and banquet will be tendered Dr. Kuyper at the New City Hotel, for which more than one hundred tickets have been sold.

Dr. Kuyper, while in Grand Rapids, visited a Latin class in one of the high schools, was invited to speak and did so, using the Latin language. The teacher thought he was using the Holland language and remarked to him that she understood the English language better than the Dutch. Evidently she understood the Latin as well as the Dutch.

From *The Holland Daily Sentinel* of 29 October 1898

This clipping reports Kuyper's lecture at the Third Reformed Church in Holland, Michigan. After a few introductory remarks, Kuyper gave the same lecture as in Princeton about "Calvinism and the Future." The reporter was afraid that the subject was too advanced for the average listener: "The subject was handled in a masterly manner, and the lecture proved to be extremely learned. . . . To thoroughly grasp the subject as discussed it was necessary for one to be versed in history – profane and ecclesiastical, – in science in nearly all of its branches and in theology. One listening to the broad survey of men and matter and the deep insight into the principles underlying human affairs today, knew at once that there was a master mind." In this lecture Kuyper once more emphasized the meaning of Calvinism for American society: "America looks forward toward a grand future but it needs the principles of Calvinism to strengthen its backbone." "[Kuyper] rejoiced to know that the Hollanders in this country were becoming Americanized. The language of America must be yours, and the country must be your country."

some rest, because this week things will be busy again in Pella and Orange City, eighteen hours by train from here. So there is no doubt that I will be home later. Otherwise it will kill me. My birthday had a most sympathetic start during the banquet. At the stroke of 12 all the guests stood up and congratulated me, and everyone sang for me. I received telegrams from Rotterdam, Amsterdam, and Leeuwarden. A letter from Jeanet[18] and a card from the editorial staff of *De Standaard*. Nothing from you. Probably forgot the date. However, I know you wish me well anyway.

The plan now is: this week Pella and Orange City, two Dutch colonies. Then the week after that, November 6–13, here in Chicago. First, 3 lectures in McCormick Seminary.[19] Second, an address to the Hollanders here (about 10,000). Third, a banquet in the Holland Club under the auspices of the Dutch consul.[20] And then I will go to Toledo, Cleveland, and Rochester. *Provided I last*. Then still Hartford, New Brunswick, Paterson, New York, Philadelphia, and then to Washington to see the President. It's enough to make one collapse. But all the enthusiasm keeps me going.

I am having a delightful stay at a beautiful hotel, with a view of Lake Michigan. An amazing city, completely rebuilt after the fire of '73, with houses 12 or 13 stories high. My hotel too. They call those houses "sky scrapers." They scrape the sky. They have all kinds of names like that. Young gentlemen who admire a lady but do not ask her are called "chair warmers." The young ladies have now organized a big association to combat this. But I must close. Give my heartfelt greetings to Groos.[21] Send my letters on

---

18 Jeannette Jacqueline Rammelman Elsevier nee Kuyper (1847–1941), Kuyper's youngest sister.

19 McCormick Seminary was a Presbyterian theological seminary, founded in 1829, which in 1859, on the initiative of the industrialist Cyrus H. McCormick, was moved to Chicago.

20 George Birkhoff, Jr. (1827–1914), the Dutch consul in Chicago (1886–1907).

21 Toward the end of October Kuyper's wife and children were staying with

to Leeuwarden[22] and Amsterdam. And now, goodbye my sweet darlings. God keep you all. Your 61-year-old husband and father.

the Groos family in Upper Norwood near London.
22 Kuyper's eldest son Herman lived in Leeuwarden.

[13]

Auditorium Hotel, Chicago
5 November 1898

Dear wife and children,

This morning (Saturday) I returned here at 9 o'clock after traveling by train for a whole day and a whole night. Needless to say, rather worn out and tired. Sleeping in trains is always troublesome, and you feel grimy. A busy week lies behind me again, but thankfully, calmer than the one before. I would not have lasted otherwise. The overexertion in Grand Rapids and Holland affected me so strongly that on Monday I actually fell ill. I broke down. Head throbbing. Nerves on edge. And irritated bowels. I didn't shut an eye all night and sent for a doctor because I had to travel by train again for a whole night to get to Pella. Thankfully he said that it was only hyperesthesia[1] and that my pulse was regular and strong. Not a hint of fever. He said *opium* was absolutely necessary and it truly revived me. Just imagine, it was the same doctor who treated Fred here. A Dutchman, Dr. De Bey.[2] A man who goes out of his way for me and personally brought me to the station in his carriage. His sister is a homeopathic doctor[3] and now she is going to look me up too.

---

1 Excessive sensitivity.
2 Hendrik de Bey (1862–1946), physician in Chicago.
3 Cornelia de Bey (1865–1948), physician in Chicago. Kuyper was a proponent of homeopathy. At the 1898 annual meeting of the Association for Higher Education on Calvinist Principles, he had argued in favor of homeopathic medicine and had suggested establishing a chair for it at the Vrije Universiteit, an idea that did not materialize until 1961. See A. Kuyper, "Is de oprichting van een leerstoel voor de homoeopathie aan te bevelen?" in *Achttiende jaarverslag van de Vereeniging voor Hooger Onderwijs op Gereformeerden Grondslag* (Amsterdam, 1898), xxxv–xli.

51

It was a long journey to Pella, and I have never traveled with a heavier heart. Pella, you see, was founded by that Rev. Scholte[4] where De Leeuw and his wife[5] used to go to church. A man of feeling, the opposite of a Calvinist. And if you visit Pella today, and you see that death, that stiffness, that boredom, that chronic dejection, and you compare that with the Calvinist colonies of Grand Rapids, Holland, and Orange City, then you can see one of the consequences before your very eyes, how deadly that sentiment is, and how vibrant Calvinism. And so no question of enthusiasm in Pella. Deadly quiet. At the meeting it was as if they were in church. No sign of life. And to add insult to injury, a guest house such that you want to turn around and leave, with a dirty and filthy lavatory in the backyard. You don't know what a feeling of relief it was to leave that village behind. And yet it was good that I visited it. The pastors understood the evil and were so grateful that I had given a push in the other direction for once. Afterwards I went to Des Moines, the capital of Iowa, where I slept peacefully,[6] and there ran into a sturdy Dutch youth who was a delight to meet. The next day I went to Orange City where I arrived on Thursday at 6 o'clock. Here everything was life and inspiration once more. Proper, refined manners. Warmth and enthusiasm. A neat guest house with Dutch waiters. And Mr. Hospers,[7] who is a member of the senate here, a man who struck the right tone. *De Heraut* is widely read here, and many declare

---

4   Hendrik Peter Scholte (1805–1868), secessionist minister serving, among others, the region of the Betuwe (1834–1847), and founder in 1847 of Pella, Iowa.

5   Presumably members of the Reformed church in Beesd, Kuyper's first pastorate (1863–1867).

6   In the light of Kuyper's experiences in Pella, compare his description of the hotel in Des Moines, in *Varia Americana*, 4: ". . . even in a city like Des Moines, the capital of Iowa, they offer you, in a beautiful hotel which is in no way inferior to our best hotels, a fine room with a bathroom on the first floor, and have you pay no more than *f*7.50, which includes three hot meals, without the obligation to drink wine."

7   Hendrik Hospers (1830–1901) was the president of the Orange City Bank and a member of the Iowa Senate (1896–1900).

that they owe their revival and energy to *De Heraut.* Jo, how wonderful it is, and [it] makes [me] so profoundly grateful. The ministers take their sermons from it. One minister had traveled a great distance by train to come and listen. The German pastors just as well as the Dutch. There was such a profoundly grateful feeling. They paid everything for me. Train to Chicago, guest house, etc., and then I received an honorarium of ƒ250 for my appearance. Oh, it gladdened my heart so in that place. And now the Chicago tour starts. Monday in Englewood for the Hollanders. Tuesday, Thursday, and Friday for the English Presbyterians in McCormick Seminary. Wednesday at the Holland Club in English again. Friday a conference with deputies. Tuesday a reception at Joldersma's. And then they ask even more. But everything is so warm and wonderful. This morning at 9 o'clock four pastors were at the train to pick me up with two carriages. The guest house here is excellent, and I now hope for a quiet Sunday.

So wonderful that it rained letters from home! This time I got two from dear Mar,[8] particularly the first [was] such a refreshing letter, one from Her,[9] one from Bram, one from Har,[10] one from Jo, one from To, and from Guy, besides letters from Hovy and others, and from our girls a card with a poem. Those good girls! And then on top of all that, another four folio pages from dear Harry, whose whole heart spoke to me. I don't know how to thank you for so much love. All the more so because I cannot answer all of them personally. I absolutely *must* rest. Right now two different groups are coming to speak to me, and those visits take so long. But do know that you have made me extremely happy. It was such bliss for my heart. Again, I send to you all, one by one, all of you together, my heartfelt and profound gratitude for this. My heart needs it. There are strings in that heart with which all the love *here* cannot strike a chord.

---

8 Cornelia Maria Johanna (Marie, Mar) Heyblom (1861–1939), the wife of Herman Kuyper.

9 See note 6:6.

10 See note 1:6.

I still cannot say very much about my return. It will surely be the end of November before I can leave America. The pressure of last month in particular forces me to be careful. I am now in my 62nd year and must take care. But in the east nothing has yet been fixed for any of the days, because I decided to drop Washington. I also have a lot of work to do here for setting up a branch of the Algemeen Nederlandsch Verbond[11] (in the Netherlands, Belgium, Transvaal, etc.), with which I have been charged and which may be useful here. I am also busy getting rid of *Wien Neerlandsch bloed* and introducing *Wilhelmus*.[12] But everything is an effort. It has to be printed, distributed, mailed. And so I toil and plod away, but I feel I am *doing something*. Something is being *done*, I don't just come and then leave, but something stays behind. The insistence upon having me is tremendous. Just as much from the American side. My journey was imperative, it was part of my life, it's a part of my task. That is why I am of good cheer and travel on quietly and calmly. Our God will bring it to pass. And already, dearest wife and darling

11 The Algemeen Nederlandsch Verbond was chartered in 1898 for the purpose of promoting ties between speakers of Dutch throughout the world. From its inception Kuyper was a member of the federation's Raad van Bijstand (Advisory Council). In connection with his trip to America he had taken with him, upon his own request, a letter from the Federation's board of directors in which it expressed its support of anything he might accomplish on behalf of the Federation in the United States. From Holland he also took along a "Constitution of the American Branch of the General Dutch Alliance."

5 *Wien Neerlands bloed* was the Dutch national anthem, written by Hendrik Tollens (1780–1856) as his entry in the competition organized in 1815 for the acquisition of a new national anthem. The song *Wilhelmus*, attributed to Marnix van Sint Aldegonde (1538–1598), did not become the official national anthem of the Netherlands until 1932. Cf. Kuyper, *Varia Americana*, 116: "*Wien Neerlandsch bloed* has had its day. If anywhere, it was out of place in America. [Its reference to] 'alien stains' insulted every family among our colonists. *Wilhelmus* on the other hand is precisely the heroic anthem that suits our colonists, most of whom are of Calvinist stock." (According to the first stanza of *Wien Neerlandsch bloed*, Dutch blood is free of "alien stains.")

children, if my guess is right, you are now home again. October 24 to Groos, staying there 14 days, makes November 7, and this will not reach you until November 15. Greetings to all our dear friends, tell Hovy that his telegrams and letters have truly done me good. Give everyone my love, kiss each other from me, and be commended to our faithful God and Father by your so loving husband and father.

[14]

My dear ones,

Once more a week of unprecedented busyness lies behind me, and unfortunately much trouble with insomnia, diarrhea, and a cold. The weather has been awful. Chicago is situated on the shores of Lake Michigan, a body of water as big as a sea, where yesterday, just outside the city, three steamships were shipwrecked. Wind, snow, rain make it truly frightening, and it is almost impossible, when perspiring during such a stressful time, to wrap up well. Luckily I have a homeopath, a female doctor, who helped me marvelously, and also brought a halt to the cold I had caught. As a result, I have been able to round off everything and leave this place with a grateful heart.

Of the friendliness and enthusiasm here in Chicago you have no idea. On Monday I gave a lengthy speech in Marlowe Hall,[1] an opera house that was packed to the rafters and where I spoke for two hours amid thunderous applause and the singing of *Wilhelmus*. All the Hollanders here still relied on *Wien Neerlands bloed*, but I put a stop to that and had it replaced by *Wilhelmus*. 2,000 copies with sheet music were printed, and handed out at the entrance. And honestly, the singing went better than I had expected. On Tuesday I gave my first lecture at McCormick College; in beastly weather, nearly an hour's drive from my hotel, and still the hall was full to the brim and enthusiastic. On Wednesday I had an honorary banquet at the Holland Society. Of course quite different people. All commercial. I had to give

---

6   In Marlowe Hall in Englewood Kuyper spoke about the calling of the Dutch in America.

an after-dinner speech there in English for three quarters of an hour. Thankfully I managed, but it's still quite a feat. Also because I did not quite feel at ease in that company. I was therefore so grateful that at the close two people came to me who said: "Oh, we are so glad, this is the first time that the glory of our Lord has preconized in our Society."

I have had to buy myself a whole new set of clothes here for parties such as these. New shirts and collars, a white waistcoat under the dress coat, and diamond buttons. I've never looked so smart, but they insist on that here, otherwise you are not considered a gentleman in circles like these. They made me an honorary member of the club. Everything went quite smoothly. *Veni, vidi, vici.* On Wednesday morning we had a "reception" with ladies and gentlemen, followed by a luncheon. Then I went to see Siegel and Kuyper's[2] big department store. Just think, with 2,500 sales clerks. Books too. And among them all the works of Dr. Kuyper. Most charming. In the evening again a lecture at McCormick. Even worse weather. Quite a blizzard. And still 4/5 full. Went quite well. But a pity that I never have a moment's rest in my room. Endless visitors. Just now a request from Chicago University to lecture there too, which I declined. I'm exhausted. Just imagine, that university was founded by one man who donated *fifteen million guilders* for it. Afterwards a meeting with the gentlemen from Iowa and Michigan and lunch at the Union Club. Then my final lecture at McCormick. And now, Saturday, a lecture at eleven o'clock at the Theological School[3] on the antithesis between Symbolism and Revelation.[4] Then lunch with

---

1   Reference to Siegel, Cooper & Company, a large dry goods store in Chicago, opened in 1887. The director Frank Cooper was born in the Netherlands—during a business trip to Europe in 1894 he visited his father in Friesland—but had Americanized his family name Kuiper after his emigration. This change to the name was common knowledge. Kuyper used Cooper's Dutch name but spelled it like his own; cf. Kuyper, *Varia Americana*, 57.

2   The Congregational Seminary in Chicago.

3   See note 17:4.

Mr. McCormick,[5] the millionaire who founded the College. Then to Pullman City to see Fredy's place of work.[6] Yesterday I talked with Mrs. Holleman,[7] the dear lady who saved Fredy. You know. Oh, I could have hugged her. A person so dear to me because of what she did for my child. She plans to write to him again soon. On Sunday I will probably stay here and dine with Mr. [Van] Schaack,[8] a rich descendant of a Dutch family dating back to the 16th century. On Monday I leave for Cleveland at 10:30. Arrive there at 7:45 in the evening. Will speak there on Tuesday in English before a deputation of 40 churches, and then travel to Niagara and the ladies of Rochester. You don't know what a wonderful, but also what an absolutely exhausting life this is. But I manage. The joy keeps me going, and I feel more and more that I was meant to be here, both for the Hollanders and for the English. They sense that I have brought them something they lacked.

It is good to know that you are home again. All of you together. That brings peace to my heart. And yet I will probably not board ship in New York before December 9, nor arrive home before Christmas. I absolutely must have my time in Washington, and with President McKinley, in particular to plead for Transvaal.[9] See if you can make out my handwriting. I do not have more time. Someone has come to see me again. Goodbye my darlings. God bless you all together. In love and devotion, your husband and father.

---

4 Cyrus H. McCormick, Jr. (1859–1936), an industrialist, son of Cyrus H. McCormick, Sr. (1809–1884), who was an industrialist and a patron of McCormick Theological Seminary.

5 Kuyper's son Frederik worked at Pullman's Palace Car Company in Pullman City from 1887 to 1890.

6 Agnes Ewan Holleman nee Steffens (1864–1929) and her husband Peter Wallace Holleman (1860–1940), a physician in Roseland, had taken Frederik Kuyper into their home in 1891 when he had become unemployed and was without adequate financial means.

7 Peter van Schaack, chairman of the Holland Society in Chicago in 1898.

8 In 1898 England threatened to annex the Boer Republic of Transvaal. Kuyper hoped that the United States could prevent England from doing so.

[15]

The Powers Hotel, Rochester
19 November 1898

My dear ones,

Again a week has passed, and also a difficult week because I unfortunately caught a cold and had a hard time of it with my head and throat. At times I felt so discouraged and tired that I thought I could not go on. There is no end to the pressure of activities. On Saturday I spoke in Chicago at the seminary of the Congregationalists, and I was extraordinarily successful with my lecture about Ritualism.[1] As he arrived, the president said to me that he would have to leave to pick up his wife from the station, but he forgot wife and station and sat and listened, nodding his head in agreement until the very end. Afterwards, lunch with Mr. McCormick, one of the wealthiest men here, who said to me, "Everywhere where you are going you make friends and now already they are looking out for your second visit." He asked whether Harry would like to come and stay with him; he would do anything for her. On Sunday it was dinner with the president[2] of the Holland Club. Most intimate. And Monday all those folks at the station and departure to Cleveland, but before that a ride to Pullman City where Fredy worked, and on to Roseland where everyone is Dutch. There I met some men from Amsterdam who in the past had had no bread to eat and now looked robust and thanked God for their prosperity. So delightful.[3]

---

1 This speech was published in Dutch and later in English; see note 17:4 below.

2 See note 12:20.

3 Cf. Kuyper, *Varia Americana*, 8: "Near Pullman-city lies Roseland, a village built up mainly by working-class people from Holland, and now you

In Cleveland everything was splendid. You will have received the program. Just imagine, the welcoming committee was formed by all the institutes for higher education from all [parts of] Ohio, and all the leading and distinguished citizens were there. First I said a few words to the Hollanders in Dutch and then [I switched to] English,[4] but my poor throat acted so strange that I spoke with a "broad accent." Nevertheless everything went well. It was a beautiful hall.[5] And afterwards "shaking hands," for pastors and professors and private individuals only, who told me that they had seen a new light. How wonderful that is. I saw nothing of Cleveland itself. I rode home quickly, took something to make me sweat, and then went to Buffalo, near the Niagara Falls. Enjoyed it tremendously. A beautiful day. Also went to Canada to see the other falls. Jubilation in my soul! Then returned and prepared myself for Rochester. I enclose the program for Rochester and newspaper cuttings.

Here especially things were ideal, but it was a risky enterprise. I had been invited by the College Women's Club. At first I was dull, but when I saw that they praised Barnevelt[6] and company to the skies,[7] I thought: I've got to go after that. The recep-

only have to apprize yourself of the lifestyle in a village such as this to see at a glance the difference that exists between our laborers in the slums and the life of American workingmen. They are less worn-out. They look physically better. Their eyes are more intelligent. Their bearing is more proud and free. They are interested in all kinds of important matters. They are well-informed about the social and political questions of the day, and are quite capable of discussing them. Much better even than the average middle-class shopkeeper who stands behind the counter in Holland."

4 Kuyper spoke about "The Political Principles of Calvinism."
5 Kuyper spoke in the Old Stone Church in Cleveland.
6 Johan van Oldenbarnevelt (1547–1619), government advocate or grand pensionary of Holland, regarded by Kuyper and his followers as an intolerant opponent of Calvinist orthodoxy.
7 The College Women's Club had studied Dutch history; cf. Kuyper, *Varia Americana*, 40: "The married and unmarried ladies of this circle take their studies so seriously that this year they chose 'The Netherlands' as their study object and had the members write about 50 'papers'; and although not one of the lecturers was of Dutch descent, they plumbed the depths

tion was magnificent. A gentleman[8] of great stature had opened his salon. A corridor and three rooms opening onto it were full of gentlemen and ladies, all in full dress (ladies in décolleté), and then I, poor sinner, had to embark upon the risky enterprise of giving an impromptu talk for two hours in English for the first time in my life. I had to dress up smartly of course. You don't get anywhere here if you don't. Full dress, white waistcoat, opera hat, white gloves. And in this state I was introduced by Miss Olive.[9] I don't understand how, but I was as calm as if I were at home, and stood up, looked calmly at all those gentlemen and ladies, and went at it, laying into Arminius[10] and Barnevelt and castigating the Club severely for renouncing "the soul of the movement": Calvinism. It went wonderfully well. I was so free, I can't understand it myself. And that went on for nearly two hours, almost without a hitch. I don't understand how I did it. I feel now that I am more used to things here and am in command of my audience. That's why a short break did not do any harm. Once you are in it you can forge ahead. Then at half past ten a reception. Papa looking smart on a kind of platform, and all those gentlemen and ladies coming forward one by one, handshake, a few words, and then home at 12 o'clock. I had not eaten yet. To bed at one o'clock. This morning a leading article for *De Heraut*.[11] Now a letter home. Then dinner again. And tonight to New York. What a life!

Tonight I could not get to sleep, so I got up and had a bath. Things went better after that. My cold has cleared up somewhat.

---

of our national history more thoroughly than is the case even with the educated women of our own country."

8 William R. Taylor, a pastor in Rochester.

9 Olive Davis, president of the College Women's Club in Rochester.

10 Jacobus Arminius (1560–1609), a Reformed theologian who argued for a softening of the Calvinist doctrine of predestination. His supporters formed the Remonstrant party in the church. Their point of view was rejected at the international Synod of Dort (1618/19).

11 This front-page article concerned an installment in the series of articles on Common Grace.

In New York I will have four days of rest. I've bought a ticket for the *Rotterdam*, which sails from New York on December 10. Don't tell anyone. I will get off at Boulogne and return home overland. Probably toward Christmas. Bram's birthday[12] as well as Too's[13] are in my thoughts. But don't ask me to write. Truly I cannot. This letter is already an effort. Believe in my love is all I can say. And now, dear wife and darling children, greetings to you, be commended to our loving Father, and think with tenderness of your weary, yet happy, father.

---

12 Bram's birthday was on November 14.
13 Cato's birthday was on November 30.

[16]

New York
20 November 1898[1]

I wrote my last letter in somewhat an exalted state of mind, being really overexerted. Therefore, my dear, in order to leave you not for a whole week in suspension, I'll tell you by this card, that I arrived safely in Fifth Avenue Hotel here, after traveling the whole night. I came here at 9 o'clock. At half past nine there was already a caller. But then I went to bed, and slept soundly till 5 p.m. After which sleep I felt quite restored and quieted, much better than I had expected. My love to all, and my best kisses for you, yours.

---

1 This letter was written in English on a postcard.

[17]

Fifth Avenue Hotel, Madison Square, New York
26 November 1898

And so, dearest wife and children, the time of my departure approaches. But I am not yet done. I have 14 busy days ahead of me, but at least the end is in sight. This coming week I have to lecture in New Brunswick and Baltimore. In New Brunswick a lecture, in Baltimore a free talk at the University Hall of Johns Hopkins University; next, a dinner in my honor in Baltimore; then to Washington, to the President and the Secretaries; and finally to the south to visit a new region where there are Dutch colonists. In the final week I have another three lectures in Philadelphia, in Hartford, and in New York. Then a few more conferences, and then on December 10, on Saturday at 10 a.m., I board the *Rotterdam*. Then I think I will travel on to Boulogne and write from there about my plans. Perhaps a lecture in London and then on to home at last.

This week has done me good. Only lectured twice. First in Paterson, and then in New York for the gentlemen of the Holland Society,[1] in English of course, after a splendid dinner. In Paterson the weather was beastly. A thick layer of snow. Yet the hall was chock-full. The committee itself was amazed by it. Thankfully I am now somewhat rested. You cannot imagine how much I slept. Well into the day, every day. But this proves that I have a healthy constitution and have not impaired my health overly much. Still, at my stage of life it's a really tough job. My cold is now practically over. The diarrhea has passed. I eat and

---

1   The Holland Society in New York, founded in 1885, was a society of
    descendants of seventeenth-century Dutch colonists in America.

drink well, and as I don't go for walks much[2] I do exercises in my room. I hereby send a speech, rolled up, that I wrote in English just now, and which I want Harry to translate into good Dutch right away, and have it published in *De Heraut*. Title: Address delivered by Dr. A. Kuyper at the Historical Presbyterian Society in Philadelphia[3] about the rapid spread of ritualism.[4] Best to translate *symbolism* as "symbolische richting" [school of symbolism] and divide it among two *Herauts* ; that will give Herman[5] some time off around Christmas. Write to him about this, and have the article in two parts published in the two *Herauts* on Christmas Day and New Year's Eve. That's when the dear boy is busiest. Professors Rutgers or Geesink[6] will proofread the piece. I have now received all your letters at regular intervals, and I thank you wholeheartedly for them. If I had more time I would write a reply to every letter and would also write on the birthdays. But that *cannot* be. I don't have a single free moment. All kinds of things to do, and my handwriting shows sufficiently that I am not yet *calm*. Just for fun I enclose a letter by Mrs. Taylor[7] from Rochester. As you can see, I was successful and have got the ladies working. They are now going to discuss Calvinism in those clubs. She is a pastor's wife. A strong woman, but who has completely gone astray.

We are in the middle of winter here. Snow, but beautifully clear winter weather, which has a good effect on me. You have no idea of the difficulties I'm having with that General Dutch

2   In Amsterdam Kuyper was used to going for a long walk every day.

3   For the Presbyterian Historical Society, see note 7:6.

4   The article was published in *De Heraut* of 18 and 25 December 1898. In 1899 an English edition of the lecture was published under the title *The Antithesis between Symbolism and Revelation. Lecture Delivered Before the Historical Presbyterian Society in Philadelphia, PA*. (Amsterdam/Edinburgh, 1899).

5   Herman H. Kuyper wrote a number of leading articles for *De Heraut* during his father's absence.

6   Wilhelm Geesink (1854–1929), professor of ethics at the Vrije Universiteit in Amsterdam (1890–1926).

7   Wife of the Rev. Taylor, see note 15:8.

Alliance. Prof. Kern[8] in Leiden asked me to organize things, and of course, now it's a point of honor to make a success of it. But is it ever difficult to get something like this done for America as a whole! And a lot of correspondence and conferences. Still, I hope to succeed. I have succeeded for the West, as you will have seen in *De Standaard*.[9] Fortunately I'm doing better than I thought I would. All in all I have now received $1,275, which is a good *f* 3,000—admittedly not enough, but with the royalties from the publications my expenses will be covered. Certainly better than I had expected. There are quite a number of Hollanders here who are also traveling on the *Rotterdam*, so that I will have more than enough company. I do hope for good weather. A calm sea journey would do me so much good. Here life is too tense, particularly as a result of the complications one has to navigate. Among the Hollanders there are all kinds of ecclesiastical and social and political differences of opinion.[10] I have to take sides, and that leads to heated discussions, and also the Americans try to exploit me politically from both sides, as you probably concluded from the clipping.

I'm sorry I cannot send you more newspapers, but when I leave a city I don't see the papers anymore of course, and there are too many of them to hold one back in particular. Moreover, the situation has changed a lot compared with how things used to be. At least two hundred gentlemen are giving lectures here that no newspaper pays any attention to, and it is a great exception that they mention me at all. The old days, when a person was included in a paper with his whole previous history, are over. In Princeton, Professor Dicey[11] of Oxford was awarded an hon-

---

8   J. H. C. Kern (1833–1917), professor of Sanskrit in Leiden (1865–1903) and chairman of the General Dutch Alliance (1898–1903).

9   See *De Standaard*, 18 November 1898, under the subtitle "Binnenland" (home affairs).

10 Cf. Kuyper, *Varia Americana*, 79–81, where he recalls the old dispute as to whether membership in a Masonic Lodge is compatible with church membership.

11 Albert Venn Dicey (1835–1922), professor of English law at Oxford and

orary doctorate at the same time as I, and he went to lecture everywhere, but not one daily paid any attention to it. I've been fortunate. But if they interview me it is not to hear all kinds of things *about* me, but to hear me out about American issues.

Now I still have to write out a speech and publish it in Dutch. If I can find the time, and otherwise in Amsterdam. And thus there comes an end to my penultimate letter. Just one more letter, and then I board ship. How wonderful that reunion will be! Particularly now that it's winter, life in hotels is so tiring. I long so much for home. And now, dearest wife and children, in thought receive a heartfelt kiss from your husband and father. We are almost back together, if God grants me a safe voyage. Be commended unto Him, and trust in the love of your wandering housemate.

Intersection of Broadway and Fifth Avenue, Manhattan. The building on the left is the Fifth Avenue Hotel, where Kuyper stayed. On the right is Madison Square.

fellow of All Souls College (1882–1909). For his observations on Kuyper in Princeton, see Peter S. Heslam, *Creating a Christian Worldview: Abraham Kuyper's Lectures on Calvinism* (Eerdmans/Paternoster, 1998), 65.

[18]

Hotel Rennert, corner Liberty & Saratoga Streets, Baltimore
2 December 1898

Dear wife and children,

On the steamship I am to travel on for twelve hours, to be back in Baltimore early tomorrow, I have found a corner of a table in order to write, and I do this because it will be impossible for me to find the time tomorrow. Again the week was busy, even though I had only one lecture, last Monday in New Brunswick. On Sunday I dined at the home of Mr. Van Norden,[1] one of New York's millionaires, a Christian, whose daughter joined the Salvation Army. His daughters were sweet, modest girls, and dinner too was modest. Soup, duck with vegetables, a sweet, and ice. In fact, I left the table half hungry because, not having anticipated such simplicity, I had taken only one portion of duck, thinking there would be other dishes too.

On Monday I lectured in New Brunswick, at the Theological School of the Dutch Reformed Church.[2] From there I went to Baltimore and Washington and stepped over into the world of officialdom, days of honoring such as I had had nowhere else. This morning I sent you a few clippings, which you will have received. There were three reasons that contributed to such an official reception. First of all, I was on my way to see President McKinley. Secondly, Van der Hoogt,[3] originally from Amster-

---

1 Warner van Norden (1841–1914), president of the National Bank of North America and a member of the Holland Society in New York.

2 The subject of this lecture was ritualism, a movement that was rapidly gaining ground; see note 17:4.

3 Cornelius W. van der Hoogt, secretary of the immigration service of the State of Maryland. In 1899 he was described in *The New York Times* as

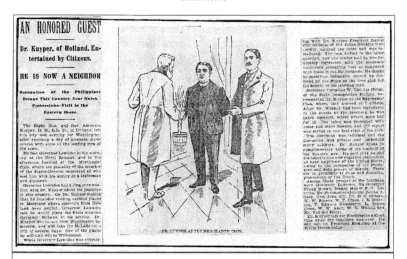

Dr. Kuyper at the Merchants' Club in Baltimore

This clipping reports that earlier in the day, while meeting with Govenor Lowndes and the president of Johns Hopkins University, Daniel Gilman: "The talk drifted to the labor question, and [Kuyper] said he was favorably impressed with the economic conditions prevailing here as compared with those in the Netherlands. He thinks co-operative industries should be fostered by the State as the true plan for the benefit of the laboring man." At the Merchants' Club: "Dr. Kuyper spoke in complimentary terms of the conduct of the Spanish war. He said that he and his countrymen now regarded themselves as near neighbors of the United States, owing to the occupation of the Philippine and Sulu groups of islands. These are in proximity to Java and Sumatra, possessions of the Dutch."

dam, moves in official circles here and had prepared everything with great tact. And thirdly, there is a new Dutch colony here with Joldersma at its head. Tuesday morning I had a meeting in my hotel with the governor[4] and his military and civilian adjutants, and with the president of the university.[5] Afterwards an elegant lunch at the governor's with all the high-ranking authorities, where the governor let me know that a state steam-

---

"the Boer agent in Washington."

4 See note 9:11.

5 Daniel Coit Gilman (1831–1908), first president of Johns Hopkins University in Baltimore (1876–1901).

er had been placed at my disposal. Tuesday evening I went to Washington, where, incidentally, I had to pay ƒ25 for my room, and Wednesday morning to the White House. I waited, in my best outfit of course, for a full quarter of an hour and was then admitted to the President, a friendly man, with whom I spoke mainly about Transvaal, because I am afraid that Transvaal will

President William McKinley

On 30 November Kuyper made a short visit to President McKinley, about whom he remarked in *Varia Americana:* "McKinley is not a statesman of the first order, but he is a man of prayer" (185).

be sacrificed for the love of England.[6] Leaving him I went to the Vice President, Mr. Hobart,[7] also president of the Senate, a man of Dutch descent. And then on to the Department of Labor,

---

6 Kuyper, during his audience with President McKinley, asked him to lift the embargo on the export of American horses to South Africa. See A. Kuyper, *Antirevolutionaire Staatkunde* (Kampen, 1915), 1:405. A year later the Second Anglo-Boer War (1899–1902) broke out.

7 Garrett A. Hobart (1844–1899), Vice President of the United States (1897–1899).

where I had a long conversation about the social question and was promised that from now on all publications on the subject would be sent to me.[8] New responsibilities for Harry.[9] In the afternoon I went on to see the Capitol, first attended a session of the Supreme Court, and returned to Baltimore in the evening. There the reporters descended on me again of course.

On Thursday I had all kinds of meetings, first with the Dutch colonists here in Maryland, with the Board of Immigration, and with the Board of Labor. All long sessions. Most distinguished. In the evening we went by ship to the south of the country to take a look at the place where the colony was.[10] Special reporters traveled with us, and a complete staff of official persons. Everything had been cabled in advance. Here I saw the country and visited with Dutch farmers. Made full inquiries. Telegrams about our visit were continually being sent to Baltimore. And when we were about to board, the ship used a searchlight to shine a light beam of some considerable length on the dark road on which we were driving. In short, nothing but official luxury. Everyone bowing and nodding. Everywhere introduced to hordes of authorities. Really *too* much. Now I hope to be back in Baltimore at 8 o'clock. Then lunch with a fabulously rich man at his country estate. Then a visit to a Negro family. And then tomorrow evening on to Philadelphia. I sent you the invitation card of the lecture I will give there on Tuesday. On Wednesday evening I have to lecture again in Hartford, near Boston. Return to New York on Thursday morning to lecture there. Then on Friday a meeting with the top brass about the General Alliance, and [will] board ship on Friday to put out to sea at 10 o'clock on Saturday. I hardly know how I'll get through it because I'm dead tired, though still in good spirits. Before I board ship I will send a postcard. Nothing more. How I managed to finish *De Heraut*

---

8 Cf. Kuyper, *Varia Americana*, 51.
9 Henriëtte Kuyper translated English texts for her father.
10 The colony lay on the peninsula between Chesapeake Bay and Delaware Bay. Cf. Kuyper, *Varia Americana*, 24.

under these circumstances, I do not know. However, I managed, but sometimes just in the nick of time, particularly as I still suffer from diarrhea, which is so tiring.

This week in particular was stressful. You have to make a good impression and converse endlessly with distinguished gentlemen. Baltimore is oh so aristocratic. And as this week comes to an end, so does this event in my life. Rich in experience and in enjoyment, and I hope not without rewards and blessings. The hurricane was awful here this week, 167 ships were wrecked off the coast. In New York you could hardly stay on your feet, and you had to wade through the snow. This probably marks the end of the worst stormy weather, so that the crossing will be calmer. May God grant it. May He guide me safely. How wonderful and rich our reunion will be! As soon as I arrive I will send a wire from Boulogne, including the place where I expect to receive a return telegram immediately. And now to conclude, my dear wife and children, may God be everything to us. Greetings to our friends. Greet Anna on her birthday.[11] Your loving husband and father.

---

11 Kuyper's eldest sister's birthday was on December 15.

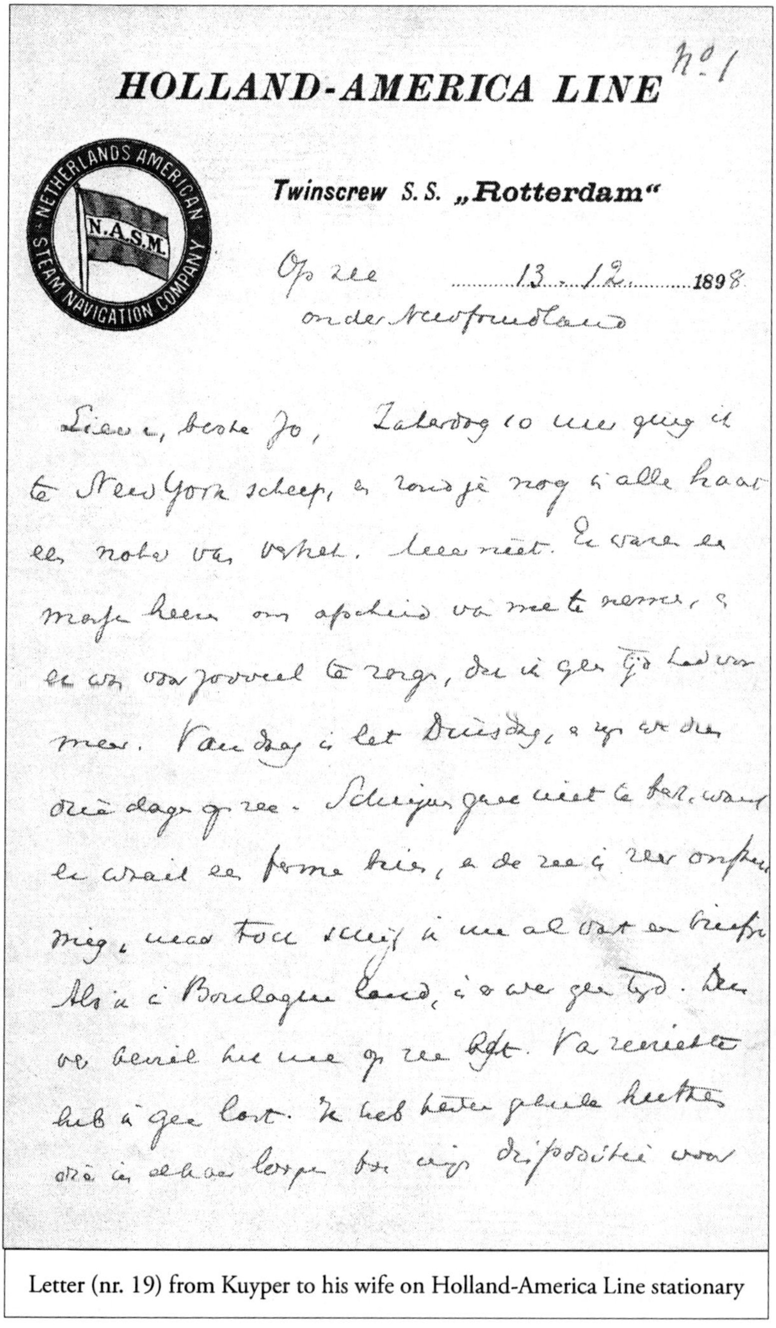

N:o 1

HOLLAND-AMERICA LINE

NETHERLANDS AMERICAN STEAM NAVIGATION COMPANY — N.A.S.M.

Twinscrew S. S. „Rotterdam"

Op zee 13.12.1898
onder Newfoundland

Lieve, beste Jo, Zaterdag 10 uur ging ik
te New York scheep, en zond je nog in alle haast
een notie van vertrek. Meer niet. Er waren er
massa's heel om afscheid van mij te nemen, en
er was nog zooveel te zorgen, dat ik geen tijd had voor
meer. Vandaag is het Dinsdag, en zijn we dus
drie dagen op zee. Schrijven gaat niet te best, want
er waait een ferme bries, en de zee is zeer onstuimig,
maar toch schrijf ik nu al vast een briefje.
Als ik in Boulogne land, is er weer geen tijd. Dan
ver beviel het mij op zee best. Van zeeziekte
heb ik geen last. Ik heb heden geheele hutten
drie in elkaar loopen tot mijn dispositie voor

Letter (nr. 19) from Kuyper to his wife on Holland-America Line stationary

[19]

On board the SS *Rotterdam* (Holland-America Line)
13 December 1898
No. 1. At sea, south of Newfoundland.

Dear Jo,

On Saturday at 10 o'clock I boarded ship in New York, and in all haste sent you word of my departure. No more than that. There was a large number of gentlemen to say goodbye to me and there was so much to take care of that I did not have time for more. Today it is Tuesday, so we have been at sea for three days now. Writing is a bit difficult because a stiff breeze is blowing and the sea is very rough, but I'll write you a short letter now already. When I go ashore in Boulogne there won't be time again. Until now I have had a good time at sea. I am not bothered by seasickness. I have two whole cabins at my disposal that open on to each other for 73 dollars. Very cheap. The table is all right. The company is not too large, and *leidlich*.[1] There is a widow (German), who went to America 5 years ago to marry there, then lost her husband again, and now without a child or anything is repatriating, lonely and forlorn. A serious, deeply sensitive woman, and it pleased me that I was able to offer her some support. Van der Hoogt, who helped me in Baltimore, is also on board, and all kinds of people who know me. The boat travels at 15 knots, and as it is over 3,000 knots to Boulogne we will probably arrive there on Tuesday morning (the 20th). My plan is immediately to take the mail boat from Boulogne to Folkestone and travel on to London, from there to Paris, and from Paris by way of Brussels to Amsterdam.

I hope to be back home a few days before New Year's Eve.

---

1 Tolerable.

Jo, how wonderful that will be, especially if the boat allows me to rest somewhat. The first two days I fell asleep as soon as I sat down. I was so exhausted and tired those last days. It had been so very busy. On Tuesday in Philadelphia a great success. Then lickety-split to Hartford in Connecticut. Gained an essential victory there. All of them anti-Calvinists, who had shrugged their shoulders, and who, after hearing me, became enthusiastic.[2] Then back to New York and there my last lecture on Thursday evening.[3] I was so glad it was over! But then only Friday remained, and that day the place was full of reporters who came for interviews, and in my hotel I had a meeting with the bigwigs for the General Dutch Alliance. Thankfully that also went well, and it is very satisfying for me that I was able to bring that difficult case, which drove everyone else to despair, to such a happy conclusion.[4] Then packed. It took me until ten o'clock that evening. And then I went for a short walk, supped, and to bed, to leave at 8 o'clock on Saturday morning, to the boat an hour away. Then answered all kinds of letters on the boat and settled money matters, and sailed at *ten o'clock*. You will probably receive the last newspaper from America at the same time as this. Take care to save those especially.

And now, my dearest wife, let me thank you wholeheartedly for writing to me so loyally and so truly *affectionately* this time. That binds us so. I now long so much. As long as I was in that frenzy I hardly had time to have such longing; but now that things have quieted down, now indeed, everything in me is long-

---

2   Kuyper spoke about "Calvinism: A Political Scheme."
3   In the Collegiate Church in New York Kuyper spoke about "A New Development of Calvinism Needed."
4   On 9 December 1898, at Kuyper's proposal, the eastern division of the American branch of the General Dutch Alliance was founded. Among those on the board of directors were Van Norden, Jacobus, Vos, Griffis, and Van der Hoogt. At Kuyper's proposal, a western division was founded on 19 July 1899 in Holland, Michigan. Among the members of that board were Dosker, Ten Hoor, and Joldersma. The eastern division proved not viable and merged with the western division in 1902.

ing, for my dear wife, my dearest children, and my wonderful work. May God give us a happy reunion. Yours.

[20]

On board the SS *Rotterdam* (Holland-America Line)
19 December 1898

No. 2. On board.

Today, dear wife, the last day of the journey. Thankfully everything went well to the end. The weather was fine every day. Only
a few people were seasick. I had not the least trouble. However,
I did not get much sleep because of the noise of the engine. Just
now we are south of Wight, where you had such a good time.
Mr. Van der Hoogt is so good as to take a suitcase and satchel of
mine,[1] and will call in person. Be nice and kind to him. He did
what he could for me in America.

I think I will arrive in Boulogne at 2 o'clock tonight. Will
sleep there, and leave for London at 12 o'clock. I think I will stay
there until Friday evening and travel to Paris on Saturday morning to look for a French lady, arrive the following Friday in Brussels and home on Saturday evening. That is the nicest evening to
arrive home. Of course I will write to you before then.

In September I forwarded a newspaper article with the title
"New Calvinism" by Dr. Horne,[2] to give to Rutgers. Ask for it
immediately, and send it to me *at once* at *Cecil Hotel*, Strand, London. In Paris my address is: Hotel Bellevue, Avenue de l'Opéra.

And now, thanks be to God that I am back in Europe. Now
for a few days to catch my breath. And then we'll see each other
again. How rich and wonderful that will be! Kiss all my darlings
from me, and you, my dearest little wife, in thought I press you
to my bosom. Your loving husband.

---

1   Bag for banknotes and such.
2   See note 4:3.

[21]

Hotel Cecil, Strand, London
21 December 1898

My dear Jo,

I cannot express how truly happy your telegram made me. I suddenly felt so very close to you, and it was as if I embraced you and gave you a heartfelt kiss. You have probably received my letters, and heard all about the sea voyage from Mr. Van der Hoogt. For you to count on my arriving Saturday was a mistake. The boat of the Holland-America Line takes 10 whole days to get to Rotterdam. So we arrived exactly on time. Only, I was sorry it was the middle of the night. I disembarked at half past three and did not get my things until a quarter past five. Being awake all night did me no good at all, so I had a bad day yesterday and still feel the effects in my head today.

That I do not return home directly is imperative. Before I return home I must get over my nervous exhaustion somewhat, and need a few days to go for walks in peace. In addition, I have to go in search of a French lady before I repatriate. How lovely for Fredy.[1] It revives me, and I have hopes for him once more. It is a most respected family. Thank you for your part in the matter up till now. Enclosed a postcard for Paulien's[2] birthday. What you wrote about the sad occurrence in the congregation is absolutely true. Satan seeks to ruin, and people don't believe it and lead a loose life. In America they fight against vice and crimes

---

1 On 2 November 1898 Frederik Kuyper had written to his parents to tell them that he had become engaged to Mary Ferguson, daughter of J. H. Ferguson (1826–1908) who lived in Padang on Sumatra and who had been the Dutch consul-general in China (1872–1895).

2 Not traced.

more deliberately, and that keeps minds alert. I have not seen Groos yet. I invited them to dinner, but he wrote that they could not make it. Now I will ask them tomorrow. I will probably not see Miss Ashton. She must not be in London.[3] On Friday or Saturday I will go to Paris, by way of Calais. Hotel Bellevue, Avenue de l'Opéra. Do not worry, my dearest, that I will be spoiled. I know to live high, but also how to live a normal life. But I dread rather the press of business that awaits me. Embrace my darlings for me, as you too are pressed to a warm heart by your loving husband.

---

3   See, however, Ethel Ashton Edwards, in H. S. S. Kuyper and J. H. Kuyper, eds., *Herinneringen van de oude garde aan den persoon en levensarbeid van dr. A. Kuyper* (Amsterdam, 1922), 177: "During the next fourteen years [after Kuyper's departure to the United States] I only saw him once—a few months later, after his return from America, when he asked me to come and dine with him in London."

[22]

Grand Hotel, Boulevard des Capucines 12, Paris
28 December 1898

My dear Jo,

Things here fell short of my expectations. As ample as the choice for English ladycompany [*sic*] was in London, so limited the choice is here. I have driven from agency to agency, but it is and remains meager. Mostly girls from lower middle class families, or elderly widows of the same background who have nothing [to offer] except that they speak French. However, through Monsieur Taunay[1] I have come into contact with Mlle. Vienot,[2] who has a large boarding school here, and she suggested a governess to me, a certain Miss Bach,[3] a lady of about 45. She is said to be very sharp and used to "terminer l'éducation," as it's known here among respectable families. She is a Protestant and accustomed to polite society. There is only one drawback. She is from Lorraine and this is noticeable in her accent, which has nothing of that soft, fluent French of the Parisians. She also created the impression of being somewhat authoritarian, a rather stout, imperative lady. If you do not want to take this on, then all that remains is a soft, timid girl of about 34 years, who chats in beautiful French but who is not as well educated. I will not make the decision here but will wait until we have talked it over first. They all ask 100 francs a month. That is the going rate here.

Tomorrow I leave for Brussels on the night train and hope to arrive home on Friday. I'll send you a telegram about which

---

1 M. Taunay, member of the Bureau Central des Associations de Presse in Paris.
2 Not traced.
3 Not traced.

train, because I don't want anyone to know. I want to be alone with my darlings. We have been separated for so long and our reunion will be so deeply meaningful. Until the day after tomorrow then. May God grant us a wonderful reunion, both from heart to heart. Much love to all. Yours, K.

Index of Names

Arminius, Jacobus 61
Ashton, Ethel 44, 79

Bach, Miss 80
Benson, Louis Fitzgerald 23
Beuker, Henricus 35, 44
Birkhoff, Jr., George 49
Boissevain, Charles 19, 25
Broes van Heekeren, Ellis 12
Broes van Heekeren, J. 12
Broes van Heekeren, Willem 12

Cleveland, Grover 41
Cooper, Frank 57

Davis, Olive 61
De Bey, Cornelia 51
De Bey, Hendrik 51
De Leeuw 52
De Vries, Henri 25
De Vries, John Hendrik 10, 11, 25, 26, 32, 37
De Witt, John 12, 26
Deen, Jacques 18, 25, 30
Del 35
Dicey, Albert Venn 42, 66
Diekema, Gerrit John 47
Dosker, Henry Elias 26, 34, 45, 47, 75

Ferguson, J. H. 78
Ferguson, Mary 78

Geesink, Wilhelm 65
Gilman, Daniel Coit 69
Green, William Henry 33
Griffis, William Elliot 21, 75
Groos 3, 49, 79
Groos family 50, 55

Heyblom, Carnelia Maria Johanna (Mar) 53
Hobart, Garrett A. 70
Holleman, Peter Wallace 58
Holleman-Steffens, Agnes Ewan 58
Horne, C. Silvester 17, 77
Hospers, Hendrik 52
Hovy, Willem 32, 53, 55
Hudson, Henry 16
Huizinga, Abel Henry 25
Hunningher, C. 5

Jacobus, Melanchton Williams 30, 75
Joldersma, Rense Henry 42, 47, 53, 69, 75

Kern, J. H. C. 66
Kuyper, Catharina Maria Eunice (To, Cato, Tokkie) 4, 34, 53, 62
Kuyper, Guillaume (Guy) 7, 24, 53
Kuyper, Henriëtte Sophia Suzanna (Harry) 2, 4, 53, 59, 65, 71
Kuyper, Herman Huber (Her) 24, 50, 53, 65
Kuyper, Jan Frederick Hendrik (Fred) 35, 47, 51, 58, 59, 78
Kuyper, Johanna Hendrika (Jo) 4, 32, 53
Kuyper, Jr., Abraham (Bram) 4, 24, 42, 53, 62
Kuyper-Schaay, Johanna Hendrika (Jo) passim

Lowndes, Jr., Lloyd 34, 69

Malster, William T. 34
McCormick, Jr., Cyrus H. 58, 59
McCormick, Sr., Cyrus H. 49, 58

McKinley, William 34, 58, 68, 70
Mokma, Gerben W. 45
Mond-Kuyper, Anna Christina
    Elisabeth 24, 72

Patton, Francis Landey 33
Paulien 78
Poppen, Jacob 11

Rammelman Elsevier-Kuyper, Jean-
    nette Jacqueline 49
Rutgers, Frederick Lodewijk 17,
    65, 77

Schaay, Hendrika Petronella 12
Scholte, Hendrik Peter 52

Taunay, M. 80
Taylor, Mrs. 65
Taylor, William R. 61, 65
Ten Hoor, Foppe Martin 36, 75
Tollens, Hendrik 54

Van der Hoogt, Cornelius W. 39,
    68, 74, 75, 77, 78
Van Heekeren, Ellis Broes 12
Van Heekeren, J. Broes 12
Van Heekeren, William Broes 12
Van Norden, Warner 68, 75
Van Oldenbarnevelt, Johan 60
Van Raalte, A. C. 46
Van Schaack, Peter 58
Van Sint Aldegonde, Marnix 54
Van Waalwijk, D. A. 30
Verwey, Isaäc 47
Vienot, Mlle. 80
Vos, Geerhardus 11, 32, 75

Warfield, Benjamin B. 11, 33
Wilhelmina, Queen 7, 13, 17, 18,
    20, 21, 30

CPSIA information can be obtained at www.ICGtesting.com
Printed in the USA
LVOW110925060412

276264LV00001B/2/P